Self Help for Women

Self-Esteem, Confidence and Assertiveness (3 in 1)

Workbook and Training in Self-Love and Self-Acceptance to Stop Doubting and be Your Confident Self

By

Maria van Noord

© Copyright 2018 - All rights reserved.

The content contained within this book may not be reproduced, duplicated or transmitted without direct written permission from the author or the publisher.

Under no circumstances will any blame or legal responsibility be held against the publisher, or author, for any damages, reparation, or monetary loss due to the information contained within this book. Either directly or indirectly.

Legal Notice:

This book is copyright protected. This book is only for personal use. You cannot amend, distribute, sell, use, quote or paraphrase any part, or the content within this book, without the consent of the author or publisher.

Disclaimer Notice:

Please note the information contained within this document is for educational and entertainment purposes only. All effort has been executed to present accurate, up to date, and reliable, complete information. No warranties of any kind are declared or implied. Readers acknowledge that the author is not engaging in the rendering of legal, financial, medical or professional advice. The content within this book has been derived from various sources. Please consult a licensed professional before attempting any techniques outlined in this book.

By reading this document, the reader agrees that under no circumstances is the author responsible for any losses, direct or indirect, which are incurred as a result of the use of the information contained within this document, including, but not limited to, — errors, omissions, or inaccuracies.

Table Of Contents

Part 1: Confidence for Women

Chapter 1: Introduction - What is Confidence?

Chapter 2: Understanding Your Current Level of Confidence

Chapter 3: How to Start Being Confident

Chapter 4: Self-Awareness - Define Your Core Values

Chapter 5: Setting Goals to Achieve Your Mission and Purpose

Chapter 6: Tips and Tricks to Build Confidence - Part I

Chapter 7: Tips and Tricks to Build Confidence - Part II

Conclusion

Part 2: Assertiveness for Women

Chapter 1: Introduction – Types of Communication

Chapter 2: Why Do We Behave the Way We Do?

Chapter 3: Current Level of Assertiveness

Chapter 4: Building Assertiveness Based On Your Core Values

Chapter 5: Change Your Inner Beliefs

Chapter 6: Communication Techniques to Practice

Chapter 7: Tools to Build Assertiveness

Conclusion

Part 3: Self-Esteem for Women

Chapter 1: Introduction - What is Self-Esteem?

Chapter 2: The Components of Building Self-Esteem

Chapter 3: Habits and How to Use Them for the Good

Chapter 4: Practical Examples

Chapter 5: Workbook

Chapter 6: Conclusion

Part 1: Confidence for Women

Simple Steps to be Confident and Attractive without Being a B*tch

Chapter 1: Introduction - What is Confidence?

Confidence is a state of mind in which you feel capable of accomplishing a task or activity with little or no problems. Confidence is a reflection of your self-belief in your capabilities and abilities. Confidence is a trait that helps you take up challenging jobs. Confidence does not mean you will succeed at every task you take up, but that you are ready to accept failures too and learn from them.

Confidence is not a static measure. It is not something you will suddenly feel after one shopping spree. It is not something you get one day, and after that, it will remain with you for the rest of your life. You don't have to feel discouraged if you get up in the morning not feeling great about yourself.

Confidence is dynamic and changes depending on many factors including skill levels, self-awareness, ability to handle failures, and more. Building and improving your confidence is a lifelong process filled with ups and downs. Developing confidence is an evolving process that never stops right through your lifetime.

Jessica Williams, the tennis star, says, *"Confidence is a journey, not a destination. Where Monday I'll feel shitty about my body, and on Tuesday I'll feel like the hottest bitch in the world, you know? I think it just ebbs and flows."*

Confidence is rooted in:

- The feeling that you will get better at things when you put in the effort to learn and practice

- The feeling that you are capable of adapting to changes in the environment

Confidence comes from feeling good about and accepting yourself the way you are. You are happy with your strengths and humbly accept your weaknesses without feeling shameful or guilty.

Why Is Confidence Important?

There is nothing right or wrong about being confident or about lacking confidence. It is only a personality trait that comes with a host of benefits and is extremely useful for success and happiness. It is not a moral issue, and therefore, don't feel guilty if you think you lack confidence. In fact, many women lose confidence for multiple reasons such as:

- Receiving undue criticism

- Surrounded by negative people

- Negative self-talk in the form of, "I'm a loser," 'I'm stupid," etc.

- Negative body image in our endeavor to synchronize our image with the expectations of society

- Failing to achieve unreasonable goals set by others

Instead of feeling guilty for losing out on confidence, feel motivated to rebuild and develop it to leverage its multiple advantages which include:

You have an enhanced sense of self-worth – Your confidence will come from increased skills and knowledge and consequent success which, in turn, enhances your sense of self-worth.

You will be more joyful than before – Confidence brings with it some amount of success and an increased ability to learn from mistakes and move on. You will not feel like a loser anymore, thereby making you more joyful than before.

You will be free of self-doubt – When you are confident, it means you know and accept your strengths and weaknesses. This helps to eliminate self-doubt from your mind because you know what you can do and what you can't.

Signs of a Confident Woman

Oprah Winfrey says, "Think like a queen. A queen is not afraid to fail. Failure is another stepping stone to greatness."

You walk with your head and chin held high – Shoulders straight and head and chin held high are the unmistakable signs of a confident woman.

You have strong perspectives – As a confident woman, you will have strong and meaningful perspectives on various aspects of life including family, work, nature, and anything else. Confidence doesn't necessarily come with high levels of knowledge about that particular topic. It comes from your ability to perceive things your way.

You present yourself well in front of people – You dress well, you talk well, you interact with people nicely, and your overall presentation reeks of confidence.

You have a predetermined set of core values – You live your life on your terms which are based on a predetermined set of core values that guide you on your life path. You don't drift along but have a deep sense of purpose in life.

You give praise heartily – When you see someone doing a good job, you have no problem recognizing their talent and giving praise sincerely. Being confident ensures that you don't feel insecure with other people's skills thereby helping you give praise wholeheartedly.

You accept criticism in the right spirit – You understand and agree that you need to work on your weaknesses and the best way for self-improvement is to listen and act on constructive criticism. This knowledge allows you to take criticism in the right spirit. Hillary Clinton said, "If you want to be a change-maker, then you must learn to take criticism seriously, but not personally."

Is Confidence Learned or Genetically Acquired?

So, the question is, are women born confident or made confident? If you put ten babies between the 1-3 years together in a room, do you think their confidence level can be easily discernible? They will all behave more or less the same way, laughing at the same things and crying for the same reasons, right? However, put ten children who are over 10 years old in a room, and you will clearly begin to see how some are more confident than the others.

So, what happened between 3 and 10 years? People are influenced by the environment of their upbringing, their caregivers' attitudes, the various lessons they learned from their interactions with others, etc. We are all impacted by what we are taught and by whom we are taught these things. The impact of these lessons is felt on our confidence levels too. We learn how and what to think of ourselves, how to behave, and what kind of self-belief we should have based on our interactions with people and the environment. All of these elements affect confidence.

These elements become part of our lives during the early stages of development, and this aspect of our development plays an important role in our level of confidence. Therefore, it can be easily concluded that confidence is a learned skill and not a genetically acquired skill.

Yet, biology could play a small role in confidence. Some people could be born with a predisposition to being confident. However, such people's only advantage is that they will find it easier to learn lessons in confidence than those who appear not to be genetically predisposed to confidence. That's it. Nothing more.

Talent is an overrated item in the modern world. Hard work can never be replaced with talent. Speak to any of the achievers of the world, and they will tell you that talent without hard work has no value whereas hard work with a seeming lack of talent can take you to the pinnacles of success.

Thomas Hardy said, *"The perfect woman is a hard-working woman, not a fine lady, not an idler; but one who uses her heart, hands, and head for her own good and that of the others."*

Confidence is also closely connected to skill-building. The more you learn and the more you practice something, the better you become at it, and your confidence grows. Remember your first piano or music class? Can you recall how difficult the lesson seemed? You almost gave up after practicing for a while.

It is possible that your mother or father who believed in your capabilities urged you to keep trying, and you followed their advice. As you practiced a particular piece of music, you realized you got better at it, and your level of confidence to play it increased significantly. Therefore, confidence comes more from repeated practice and efforts rather than being acquired genetically.

Being Confident Vs. Having Confidence

The next question we tackle is "what is the difference between 'being confident' and 'having confidence?" 'Having confidence' is what you feel within you whereas 'being confident' is what others see of you.

For example, if you are giving a presentation to your colleagues, and you haven't prepared as well as you normally do, you might not have confidence in your present condition. However, your colleagues are already aware of your capabilities, and if you can 'be confident' in front of them, you just might pull off the presentation reasonably well backed by some amount of knowledge.

Another example of 'being confident' can be seen in some people who can put up a front of confidence despite knowing they don't 'have confidence' within themselves. They could use their gift of the gab to get away from tricky situations and appear confident in front of other people even though their skills are insufficient for real confidence.

Typically, women who 'have confidence' appear naturally confident in front of others. Those appear confident may not be able to keep the façade for long because the inner real self will soon reflect in outward behavior. So, it is important to have confidence by building skills so that you can be confident always.

Confidence and Self-Esteem

Confidence and self-esteem are related deeply, and yet are quite different from each other. Typically, self-esteem and confidence are directly proportional to each other. However, there are cases when they need not be aligned. For example, Emma Watson, the actress who played the role of Hermione Granger in the Harry Potter series and became a Hollywood star, oozed confidence in her role and won a lot of critical acclaim for her confident acting skills. However, she admitted to having self-esteem issues.

Self-esteem comes from a sense of self-worth. If your answer to the question, "Do I believe I am a worthy individual?" is yes, then your self-esteem is at a respectable level. But, if you are uncomfortable answering that question or are reeling in self-doubt, then you could be facing issues in that aspect.

Self-esteem is an identity issue and does not change across the different aspects of your life. If, for example, if you have a high level of self-esteem as a mother, then it is quite likely that you have the same high level of self-esteem in your office.

Confidence, on the other hand, can vary in different spheres of your life. You could be a confident mother but could lack confidence at your office and be uncertain of certain skills needed to grow and develop your career. Confidence is more an external trait that can be seen or felt by others whereas self-esteem is more an internal trait known only to you, and perhaps a few close friends.

Confidence in a particular skill can be built through the continued practice of that skill whereas the development of self-esteem is more difficult and requires you to change your overall perspective of yourself.

Confidence and Assertiveness

Confidence breeds assertiveness. But, the two are different too. Assertiveness must be necessarily showcased to the outside world whereas confidence does not have to be showcased. To be assertive, you have to talk and interact with people whereas confidence does not necessarily need to be expressed. You can feel confident about your skills and capabilities, but you don't have to show it to the outside world whereas assertiveness has to be expressed.

Chapter Summary

Confidence is knowing and accepting your strengths and weaknesses without being arrogant. Confidence is a personality trait that can be learned and mastered, and its multiple benefits can be leveraged to lead a more fulfilling and meaningful life than before. Confidence, self-esteem, and assertiveness are deeply connected and yet have many differences.

Chapter 2: Understanding Your Current Level of Confidence

Do you know your current level of confidence? It is important to know this so that you make informed choices about how to make positive changes in your life. This chapter is therefore dedicated to self-assessment quizzes and questionnaires which will help you gauge your present level of confidence so that you can make necessary alterations in the right direction.

Q1. When I am given a project report to do, I know where exactly I will find the required information.

1. Never   2. Sometimes   3. Very often   4. Always

Q2. Based on my lessons learned at college, I am confident I can do a great job in the workplace.

1. Never   2. Sometimes   3. Very often   4. Always

Q3. I like to take calculated risks.

1. Never   2. Sometimes   3. Very often   4. Always

Q4. I like to take up difficult challenges.

1. Never   2. Sometimes   3. Very often   4. Always

Q5. There are times when I may not know the answer to a question immediately. But I know where to find the required information.

1. Never	2. Sometimes	3. Very often	4. Always

Q6. I can confidently help my colleagues with any doubts in the workplace.

1. Never	2. Sometimes	3. Very often	4. Always

Q7. I confidently help my kids with their science and math homework even though I am not highly qualified.

1. Never	2. Sometimes	3. Very often	4. Always

Q8. Are you confident about appearing on a TV reality or quiz show?

1. Yes	2. I don't know	3. No

Q9. Would you give a big speech at your best friend's wedding about her?

1. Yes	2. I don't know	3. No

Q10. Do you think you are a positive individual?

1. Yes	2. I don't know	3. No

Q11. Do you let fear stop you from accepting risky ventures?

1. Never	2. Sometimes	3. Very often	4. Always

Q12. Have you ever disagreed with your seniors and bosses?

1. Never	2. Sometimes	3. Very often	4. Always

Q13. Would you contradict your boss or her boss if you believe you are doing the right thing and she is making the wrong choice?

1. Yes   2. I don't know   3. No

Q14. Do you believe that attack is the best form of defense?

1. Never   2. Sometimes   3. Very often   4. Always

Q15. Are you confident of crossing a busy highway?

1. Yes   2. I don't know, I have never tried   3. No

Q16. Would you take the ferry to an island even if you heard the weatherman say a storm was expected?

1. Yes   2. I don't know   3. No

Q17. Suppose you were asked to choose between two tasks by your boss. Would you take the more difficult one because you like to be challenged?

1. Never   2. Sometimes   3. Very often   4. Always

Q18. Do you believe you are more intelligent than the average worker in your office?

1. Yes   2. I don't know   3. No

Q19. Would you consider unraveling a woolen sweater with an intention to learn the stitches and then stitch it back?

1. Yes   2. I don't know   3. No

Q20. Are you impressed with orators and wish you could speak with such confidence too?

1. Yes   2. I don't know   3. No

Q21. Suppose you are alone at home with your kids as your husband is traveling. You hear a sound coming from the kitchen in the dead of night. Would you leave your bedroom to investigate?

1. Yes   2. I don't know; hope I don't have to face such as a situation   3. No

Q22. Do you do things that you don't really like just to keep others happy?

1. Never   2. Sometimes   3. Very often   4. Always

Q23. If your husband criticized you in front of your friends, would you raise your voice against such behavior?

1. Never   2. Sometimes   3. Very often   4. Always

Q24. Suppose you are invited to a party and that handsome hunk on whom you have a huge crush is also there. Would you walk up to him and let him know your feelings?

1. Never   2. Sometimes   3. Very often   4. Always

Q25. Do you feel happy about your talents and capabilities?

1. Never   2. Sometimes   3. Very often   4. Always

Q26. When you talk to people, do you confidently make eye contact with them, even if it is someone you are not particularly fond of?

1. Never   2. Sometimes   3. Very often   4. Always

Q27. When you have to say no to your children, do you look them in the eye and tell them no backed with valid reasons?

1. Never   2. Sometimes   3. Very often   4. Always

Q28. Suppose you went to a party, and someone misbehaved with your best friend, would you confidently tell the person to back off?

1. Never   2. Sometimes   3. Very often   4. Always

Q29. Are you happy your present levels of skills and knowledge?

1. Yes   2. I don't know   3. No

Q30. Do you need people to constantly praise you to feel good about yourself?

1. Never   2. Sometimes   3. Very often   4. Always

Q31. Do you get out of your comfort zone and try new things easily?

1. Never   2. Sometimes   3. Very often   4. Always

Q32. Are you excited about learning new things?

1. Never   2. Sometimes   3. Very often   4. Always

Q33. Do you forgive yourself for your mistakes?

1. Never   2. Sometimes   3. Very often   4. Always

Q34. Do you have your own set of core values and live by them?

1. Never 2. Sometimes 3. Very often 4. Always

Q35. Are you ready to bear the consequences of your actions and behaviors?

1. Never 2. Sometimes 3. Very often 4. Always

Q36. Are you happy with the way you manage your finances?

1. Never 2. Sometimes 3. Very often 4. Always

Q37. Do you balance your time and energy between your family and work, and also keep some free time for yourself?

1. Never 2. Sometimes 3. Very often 4. Always

Q38. Do you think you present a confident profile whether you are sitting, standing, or walking?

1. Never 2. Sometimes 3. Very often 4. Always

Q39. Do you choose your clothes with care and ensure you feel comfortable in them?

1. Never 2. Sometimes 3. Very often 4. Always

Q40. Do you usually feel positive and happy?

1. Never 2. Sometimes 3. Very often 4. Always

Self-Discovery with a Partner

Taking the help of a trusted partner is a great way to understand your current level of confidence. This exercise is a joint project that requires you to pair up with a good friend or even your life partner. First, think of an imaginary situation that requires you to be confident. For example, you could think of giving that speech at your best friend's wedding. Now, make detailed notes of the following elements basing your answers on that imagined situation:

Your emotions: will you be confident or nervous? Why?

_____

Friend's comments_____

What will you do about your emotions?

_____

Friend's comments_____

What will be your level of readiness? Would you have done a better job if you had time to prepare?

_____

Friend's comments_____

What if the audience was a smaller lot? Will your confidence level alter? How?

_____

Friend's comments_____

Answer honestly and after some thought. Your partner must do the same thing. She or he could have a different situation and a different set of questions too. Also, you can choose your own situation if the above situation does not suit your self-discovery process.

Next, give your notes to your friends, and let them read it and make their own comments in the 'friend's comments' place. Ask if they agree or disagree with your observations. Ask them to add comments that you could have missed out while answering the questions. You do the same for your friend.

This partnership will help you understand whether your outward appearance matches your internal feelings and emotions. If, for example, you had written that you would be nervous to give the speech, and your friend disagreed, then, perhaps, you are coming across as more confident than you are feeling. Think about these conflicting thoughts for a while and find out whether you are underestimating your capabilities or whether you are pretending to be confident even though you are nervous. Explore more self-awareness questions in such cases. For example:

Am I more skilled or less skilled than my outward profile?

Why do I see myself differently from how others see me?

In cases where your line of thought matches with that of your friends, then you get a fairly accurate idea of your current level of confidence.

Chapter Summary

The self-discovery activities in this chapter will help you gauge your current standing when it comes to confidence. Answer each question honestly to get accurate results using which you can plan your confidence-building path.

Chapter 3: How to Start Being Confident

What is the first step to making any positive change in your life? It is nothing but your decision to take the first step. Chloe Neill, in her highly popular book Midnight Marked, says, *"They blew out a breath and did the thing all heroes must do—they took that terrifying first step."* The first step of a new journey might appear terrifying, but, once it is taken all the following steps simply happen in real-time when you are totally immersed in the experience of the journey.

So, the journey to developing confidence starts with your decision to change today, and make all changes needed to build confidence every day from today. Start with the thought, "Today, I am confident, and I will endeavor to be confident every day."

Confidence building is not a one-time exercise. It is an ongoing process that requires you to be in a constant flux of learning and mastering new skills. Make a list of the skills you need to learn to increase confidence. Take one skill at a time and learn to practice it until you become a master. The most crucial element to be in a continuous state of learning is to have a growth mindset.

Growth Mindset

So, what is a growth mindset? Carol S. Dweck, a psychology professor, and researcher at Stanford is credited with the coining of two terms namely growth mindset and fixed mindset to discern between successful and unsuccessful people.

Unsuccessful people typically tend to have a fixed mindset in which they believe that their talents, intelligence, and capabilities are fixed and cannot undergo change no matter what you do. Driven by this belief, fixed mindset people don't attempt to achieve success. They just accept what comes their way and complain and whine.

Successful people, on the other hand, have a growth mindset which means they know that their present level of talents, intelligence, and capabilities are not fixed, and if they work hard and commit themselves to improve themselves, things can definitely change for the better.

Here are some differences between the growth and fixed mindsets:

- People with a fixed mindset tend to avoid taking up challenges, and this attitude blocks their path to success.

Growth mindset people, however, embrace challenges and treat them as opportunities for growth and learning. They are warriors who love a good fight irrespective of whether they fail or succeed.

- People with a fixed mindset either ignore or scorn criticism. They will not listen to any kind of criticism and avoid people who try to help them grow; another important reason for such people not to be able to develop their strengths.

Growth mindset people accept criticism in the right spirit and learn from it thereby growing with each new constructive feedback. In fact, people with a growth mindset are pleased to receive feedback and are thankful to people who take efforts. Learning from feedback is one of the primary reasons for the growth mindset for people to achieve success.

- Fixed mindset individuals believe that intelligence and talent are fixed. So, if their intelligence level is at one particular stage, then they believe it cannot move forward. As per the fixed mindset people, dumb people remain dumb, and clever people remain clever. 'Faults cannot be amended,' is what such people think. Here is what Confucius had to say about faults, *"The only real fault is to have faults and not to amend them."*

Growth mindset individuals have a strong belief in people's ability to build and develop their intelligence, talents, and skills through learning and practice. Such people are ever-ready to imbibe and learn new knowledge and skills.

- People with a fixed mindset don't try very hard and give up after the first or second, failed attempt. Such people refuse to learn from their failures.

Growth mindset individuals never give up and work hard to get better after every failure. They put the learning from their past failures to try again, and they persist until they achieve success. Margaret Thatcher said, *"You may have to fight a battle more than once to win it."*

- Fixed mindset people are envious of other people's success driven by their lack of self-belief and confidence.

Growth mindset individuals happily accept other people's achievements and success because such people know that if tried hard, they can achieve success too. Therefore, they don't grudge other people their success and happiness.

So, question yourself and see if you are a woman with a fixed mindset or growth mindset. If you are a victim of low confidence, then it is quite likely that you have a fixed mindset as it is a significant contributor to low confidence. The next step after making the decision to become confident is to develop a growth mindset.

Tips to Develop a Growth Mindset

Here are some tips you can put into practice straight away to develop a growth mindset:

Learn something new daily – Make it a point to pick up some new bit of knowledge daily. Listen to podcasts while commuting to work or read an article about a personal concern you have, or simply learn to sing one line from your favorite song.

Remember, learning is not getting it perfect the first time. Learning is only a way to tell your brain that new data is coming in and to be ready to imbibe and absorb it for future use. Knowledge is power in modern times. Never let a single day go by without learning something new.

Don't depend on anyone to learn anything. Today, information is at your fingertips, thanks to the ever-expanding world of the internet. Find online classes, read up articles, speak to people who are skilled about what you want to learn, and more. You can also engage with new people as often as you can to get new perspectives on life and its vagaries.

Surround yourself with positive-thinking people – Jim Rohn, the world-renowned motivational speaker and author of self-help books, says, *"You are the average of the five people you surround yourself with."*

So, if you want to build your growth mindset, surround yourself with people who have a growth mindset. People you interact with have a significant impact on your moods, behaviors, and way of life. Therefore, being with people who have a fixed mindset when you are looking to build your growth mindset will be counterproductive for success.

Challenge your fears – Fear can be so crippling that you can be frozen at the moment and you are unable to do or even think anything. Taking up any challenge calls for challenging your fears. The fears can be because of many reasons including fear of failure, fear of becoming unpopular, fear of being disliked, fear of losing love, and more.

Eleanor Roosevelt said, *"You gain strength, courage, and confidence by every experience in which you really stop to look fear in the face. You are able to say to yourself, 'I lived through this horror. I can take the next thing that comes along.'"*

It was her courage to face her fears that helped the former First Lady become a leader in her own right and participate and bring to fruition multiple benefits for the good of humanity in general and women in particular.

Never be afraid of making mistakes – Mistakes are not the end of the world. In fact, they are important for achieving success. Speak to any achiever of the world, and she will tell you that making mistakes helped in her learning and development far more than successes. Mistakes:

- Increase our desire to learn.
- Help us be more compassionate towards ourselves and towards others.
- Free us from debilitating fears and self-doubts empowering us to take increased risks.

- Reboot and rejuvenate our motivation levels which usually fade and get lost in the din of our daily grind.

When you try a new venture, be prepared that things will go wrong, and you will have to battle your external and internal demons to overcome the difficult times. But the efforts will be worthwhile because, at the end of an exercise, your confidence level will get a significant boost.

Learn and Practice New Skills

One of the primary reasons for low levels of confidence is the lack of sufficient skills. Identify the areas in which you lack skills, and work hard to learn and master these skills; a sure-shot way to build your confidence. Here are some tips on how to learn and master new skills:

Keep a curious attitude – Curiosity is a crucial element for enhancing knowledge and skill levels. If you have heard about a new thing in your office that you know will add value to your professional growth plans, then go home, and do plenty of research and learn more about that topic.

Ask why, what, how, when, and more such questions. Find answers to these questions and continue to garner information until your curiosity on the topic is completely satisfied. Don't take what one or two people or sources said to you for granted. Find information from multiple sources, and ensure you have different perspectives about the concerned subject.

The mastery of skill comes when you take a multipronged approach to learn it. When you become a master at something, people will flock to you for advice, answers, suggestions, etc. Consequently, your confidence gets a big boost.

Increase your versatility quotient – Try and skill yourself at many things. Learn to be good at your office work, learn to be a good cook, learn to be a great parent, learn some music, and read up and collect information about trending issues.

When you are skilled at many things, you can participate in any conversation with people of all ages, gender, race, and community. This wide-reaching attitude to involve yourself with multiple skills will help you be sure of yourself in many situations thereby building your confidence.

It is not necessary to be a master at everything. But it is essential that you know the basics of as many things as possible. This way you can participate in a group conversation, learn more from discussions, and help you to feel included and not excluded from the group.

Identify role models and mentors – Role models help you set a standard for yourself and give you a tangible goal of where you want to reach. Having role models make it easy to grow, learn, and develop your skills because you know where you want to reach.

While role models are people you want to copy, mentors are people who can help you achieve your dreams. Mentors don't hesitate to tell you when you are straying from your chosen path. They will not hesitate to give constructive criticism because they are your well-wishers.

Sometimes, role models and mentors can be the same person. For example, if you want to be like your mom, then she could be your mentor also, teaching and instructing you on your path. However, if you want to be like Michelle Obama, then you might have to find someone closer to you to be your mentor and well-wisher.

Chapter Summary

In this chapter, the benefits and importance of a growth mindset for building confidence were discussed. You also learned why and how you must work towards learning and practicing new skills to become a master at it.

Chapter 4: Self-Awareness - Define Your Core Values

Valuable people add value to your life. Your partner, children, friends, parents, boss, and others influence the way you think and behave. These people act as a guide in your life lighting up your chosen path, so you know you are taking the right direction to your dream destination. How are these people in your life a guiding light?

Let us take an example of your children. You value them a lot, and one of your life goals is to give them a sound education so that they grow up to be proud and responsible adults. So, you choose the neighborhood to live in based on the quality of schools in the given area. You will be willing to travel a long distance to your work as long as your children get to go to the best school. Therefore, many of your choices are based on the value and your priority of the various people in your life.

Like this, core values are the traits or qualities that guide you in your life path. They dictate your actions and behaviors. Suppose one of your core values is honesty. Then, when you are in a situation wherein you must make a choice between telling the truth and telling a lie, you will be guided by your core value to stick to the truth making it easy for you to make the right decisions.

Core values also called personal values not only make life worthy of living and uplift your morality but also form the driving force for your purposes and goals. Sheila Murray Bethel, one of the most influential business speakers today says, *"You are the storyteller of your own life, and you can create your own legend, or not."* So, it is up to you to create your personal values.

Core values define you, your personality, and what you stand for. They are life principles that you believe in deeply and are typically inherent in your psyche. You merely need to discover them. Core values become the guiding light of your life. When you don't know your core values, then it is tough to plan and live a life that you want.

Core values act as a compass to accurately show how to choose, live, operate, and behave to achieve your life purpose. They are your internal navigation system using which you process all your life choices and decisions. They become your standards for morality and competence. Core values are what you are ready to die for, and hope that you will be remembered for them when you are not on this earth anymore.

Recall an experience in your life that made you feel squeamish or deep down you knew that something was wrong. What were the emotions in your mind? Those negative feelings would invariably have been because your actions and behaviors were not aligned with your core values. Psychology experts opine that most often we feel excessive stress and anxiety when our actions and behaviors are incongruent with our inner values.

There are hundreds of core values available. However, most of us live our life aligned with the top 5-10. There are times when core values in your life could change and shift. You could unwittingly pick up core values from your family, religion, friends, school life, the outside world through print and social media, your role models, etc.

Core values are relatively unchangeable and remain the same for sustained periods of time. However, please know that it is perfectly okay to make changes to your core values by deleting those that don't make sense anymore or by adding those that have gained importance in your life.

Characteristics of Core Values

How do you define the core values of your life? What are the guiding principles of this exercise? Here are some attributes of core values that will help you arrive at your personal list.

- Core values should be practical to apply. You must not only know the techniques of how to use it but also know in what context to use it.

For example, suppose one of your core values is integrity. In an office scenario, when something goes wrong, then this core value should drive you to report the matter to the seniors. However, in a home scenario, if you are trying to get your toddler to eat something and want to use some form of filler (which could be the boogie-man, etc.), then this really does not come in the way of your core values, right?

- There should be a judgmental element in each of your core values which means it should carry your idea of what is wrong, right, or desirable.

Each person's core values form a unique set. They are like fingerprints of the concerned individual, and rarely, match perfectly with someone else's.

- Core values should be implementable irrespective of the physical state you are in. For example, you cannot really have physical fitness as a core value because it requires you to be in such a particular physical condition that allows you to implement this value. If you are sick and bedridden or stuck to one place for any reason whatsoever, physical fitness might not be implementable.

On the other hand, integrity or honesty can be implemented no matter in which condition you are in. You can display honesty even from your sickbed.

- Core values should be independent of external factors. For example, popularity cannot be a core value because you need the help of other people to like you to achieve this.

Self-Assessment Exercise to Identify or Define Your Core Values

How do you go about identifying which of the core values (from over 400) define you? Some of the core values include discipline, love, honesty, prudence, integrity, ambition, fun, health, friendship, respect, balance, family, and many, many more. For most of us, core values are typically inherent, and we unwittingly display them in our actions and behaviors. This exercise is only to help you discover these core values and label them appropriately to increase self-awareness. Here are some tips for that:

What were the five top successes and/or happy experiences in your life? – Give a name to each of these successful experiences and answer the questions given below for all of them:

Write in detail what happened in the event. When did it happen? How old were you? Who were the other people who were part of that experience? Write detailed descriptions.

- What emotions were ruling your mind and spirit in that successful or happy experience?

- What were your thoughts?

- What were the core values that were predominantly being played at that time? If the experience happened when you were very small, then it is highly likely you did not know the concept of core values then. However, now when you recall those beautiful memories, the predominant core values will come to you easily.

—

What were the worst failures and/or unhappy experiences in your life? Take the top five – Write down answers for the same set of questions as for the happy experiences except the last one which will now be, "What were the core values you believed you suppressed during these events?" So, here is a template of the worksheet for the worst five experiences in your life:

Write in detail what happened in the event. When did it happen? How old were you? Who were the other people who were part of that experience? Write detailed descriptions.

What emotions were ruling your mind and spirit in that

unsuccessful or unhappy experience?
_____

What were your thoughts?
_____

What were the core values that were suppressed at that time?
_____

Next, identify your code of conduct – For this, you must ask yourself these questions:

- After my basic life needs including food, clothing, and shelter are taken care of, what are the elements that are essential to make my life meaningful?

- What are those elements of life without which I might survive but not be able to live a fulfilling life?

Here are some examples to help you understand what your code of conduct can be:

- Nature and its beauty
- Vitality and health
- Learning
- Adventure and excitement
- Creativity

Collect all the similar values together – From the answers to the above questions, you will get a list of core values that hold the top spot in your life. Now, the list is likely to be long and unwieldy. Combine and bunch together similar core values that mean the same thing. For example:

- Achievement, accomplishment, productivity, ambition,

and other similar ones can be combined.

- Generosity, altruism, helpful, goodness, and other related values can also be kept together.

So, now your list will be easier to manage. Give one label to each bunch of similar core values. In the above two examples, the first set can be labeled as result-oriented, and the second can be called service-oriented. From this list of core values, choose the top few only.

It is important to keep your core values list between 5 and 10. If the list has less than 5 elements, then it is likely that all the important aspects of your life are not covered. If the list has more than 10 elements, then it will become difficult to track them.

The next thing to do is to rank your core values list. This might take more time than you think because ranking items that look equally important can be a challenging task. Here is a little tip. Revisit your good and bad experiences and see if you can identify the intensity of the emotions and thoughts that made up each of the experiences. The more the intensity, the higher it's ranking.

After you have set up your core values list, and have ranked them in order of importance, make sticky notes of them and paste them in all visible places. This will help you to instill your core values repeatedly into your psyche making sure you can recall them whenever you have to make decisions in life.

Chapter Summary

This chapter taught you the importance of having a clearly defined set of core values with which you can lead your life more meaningfully than before. You also got a user-friendly template along with basic instructions (which you can tweak to your requirement) on how to identify and define your core values.

Chapter 5: Setting Goals to Achieve Your Mission and Purpose

So, you know your core values, and you have made sure they are deeply instilled in your mind. Now, you should use them to create life purposes and goals for yourself. Having purposes and goals helps you to lead a more fulfilling and meaningful life than before.

For many of us, finding our purpose can be quite a challenging activity. However, we must endeavor in that direction. Barbara Hall, the famous American novelist, television writer, singer-lyricist, says, *"The path to our destination is not always a straight one. We go down the wrong road, we get lost, we turn back. Maybe it doesn't matter which road we embark on. Maybe what matters is that we embark."*

Significance and Importance of Life Purpose and Goals

Winston Churchill said, *"It's not enough to have lived. We should be determined to live for something."* Having a life purpose that is divided into time-bound goals gives you multiple benefits. Here are some of them:

Purpose gives your life meaning and value – Unlike animals, human beings need to have meaning in our lives. We cannot simply eat, sleep, reproduce, die, and all the things that other living beings do, and find happiness and contentment. Our nature is primarily attuned to find purpose. A purposeless life is meaningless which, in turn, results in hopelessness and insignificance for you as an individual. A famous quote on life purpose goes like this, *"A life purpose is the purpose of life."*

Identifying and knowing your purpose simplifies your life – Your life purpose becomes your standard which helps you determine which activities are important and which are not. Discarding activities not aligned with your purpose clears all clutter resulting in making your life simple and lightweight.

You will not feel the burden of extra weight on yourself when you align your life path with your purpose. Additionally, decision-making is made simpler than before, and you will allocate time and energy appropriately without wasting them on unrelated and wasteful tasks.

Your purpose gives you focus and prevents you from straying from your chosen path – Having a predetermined purpose in life gives you focus. You know where you need to reach, and the goals you make for yourself to reach there will provide you with a clear pathway ensuring you keep your body, mind, and spirit focused on your purpose.

In the absence of a clear purpose, your energies and resources will be scattered all over, and you will not be able to achieve anything. Also, having a purpose keeps you from straying. For example, if your purpose in your career is to become the head of your local office, then your path will consist of small steps leading to that final career goal. Every time you are tempted by an activity that is counterproductive to this final purpose, your mind will alert you, and prevent you from straying.

Your purpose prevents you from procrastinating – When you know you have to reach a particular goal within a certain time, your mind will raise the alarm every time you indulge in some procrastinating activity. Suppose you have a first date with that handsome hunk at 8 pm at a restaurant near your home. Here's what you will do:

- Make sure you leave the office by 6 in the evening and catch the commute back home.

- Go straight to your wardrobe to decide what to wear.

- Then, quickly go to the bathroom, and take a shower.

- Change, spend some time wearing makeup, and looking good.

- You are ready by 7:30.

- You then walk or get a sibling to drop you off at the restaurant a little before 8.

While you were deeply engaged in these activities, it is highly likely that you had distractions such as social media and email notifications or a call from a close friend, etc. However, the goal of being at the restaurant by 8 pm ensured you did not procrastinate and stayed away from all those distracting activities that took you away from your goal.

You may have done the entire exercise without even realizing how focused you were on your goal. That is how deeply-embedded goals keep you on track and prevent you from engaging in distracting procrastinations.

Therefore, it is imperative you find your life purpose, and then divide it into yearly, monthly, weekly, and daily goals so that you can keep track of them minutely and ensure you achieve your final purpose.

Self-Discovery Questions before You Set Goals

You must find your own purpose in life. No one can force you to accept a purpose. You must choose it of your own free will so that it helps you leverage all the benefits listed above. If someone else gave you your life purpose, then it cannot be called so. It only means you are leading someone else's life and not your own.

Venus Williams, the tennis superstar, says, *"I don't focus on what or who I am up against, I only focus on my goals, and the rest takes care of itself."*

Before you set down to write your purposes and goals in life, answer these self-reflective questions. You will find your goals hidden in your answers.

What do you enjoy doing the most in your workplace and at home?

_____

What do you want more of?

_____

What is your current status? For this, you should write down your current qualifications, your job description, your role at home, etc. You should also include how you achieved these things.

_____

Where do you see yourself 5-10 years from now? For this, you should write goals you want to achieve (along with reasons) in your professional and personal life.

———————————————————————

What are you going to do to achieve the goals you have set for yourself? Do you have to take any classes? Do you need help in any other form? How do you plan to seek help from the concerned people? Make detailed notes of your plans. This will be your 5- or 10-year plan depending on the time horizon of your life purpose. These plans will be converted and broken down into yearly, monthly, weekly, and daily goals.

———————————————————————

How will you measure your progress? What are the metrics you will use?

———————————————————————

Daily Goals Worksheet for Women

Before retiring to bed each night, complete this daily goal template. It could become your daily to-do list:

My goal for tomorrow is?

———————————————————————

What are the things I need to do to achieve my daily goal?

———————————————————————

Here are some classic examples for women that you should include in your daily goal list:

Go for my morning exercise or yoga (which could be part of your physical fitness purpose)

- Eat a healthy breakfast without fail.
- Meditate for 5 minutes before leaving for work.
- Complete the set tasks in the workplace.
- Spend some quality time with family.

Weekly Goals Worksheet for Women

Typically, goals for the week should be set on Sunday. However, if you want to keep Sunday totally free for yourself and your family, then make sure you complete this template by Saturday evening.

My goals for this week are:

_____

What are the things I need to do to achieve my weekly goal?

_____

Monthly Goals Worksheet for Women

My goals for this month are:

_____

What are the things I need to do to achieve my monthly goals?

_____

Yearly Goals Worksheet for Women

My goals for this year are: (your new year resolutions could come here; just ensure that these resolutions are aligned with your initial purpose).

_____

What are the things I need to do to achieve my yearly goals?

_____

Chapter Summary

This chapter contained ideas and insights into having purpose and goals in life. You read about the importance and benefits of goal-setting. The chapter also includes self-discovery questions which will help you arrive at your goals and daily, weekly, monthly, and yearly goal-setting templates for your use.

Chapter 6: Tips and Tricks to Build Confidence - Part I

What tips and suggestions are available to build confidence? This chapter and the next are dedicated to giving you valuable tips on how to build confidence.

Affirmations for Confidence

What are affirmations? Affirmations are positive statements that help in motivating and enhancing the positivity aura within and around you. Affirmations are short sentences that you repeat to yourself daily to help you achieve something or, sometimes, to simply make you feel better.

Louise Hay is one of the most influential proponents of positive affirmations. Each one of the chapters in her bestselling self-help book titled *'You can heal your life'* begins with a positive affirmation. Affirmations empower you to work towards making your dreams a reality.

Benefits of Affirmations

- Daily affirmations increase your ability to discern between positive and negative thoughts and facilitate the keeping out of negativity from your mind.
- When you repeat an affirmation daily and work towards your dreams, your actions and thoughts are synchronized with each other resulting in resonating

effects of your efforts. Affirmations increase your levels of focus and motivation.

- Affirmations are aligned with the law of attraction. The more you affirm a positive thought to yourself, the more you will attract people and resources needed to make the thought a reality.

- Affirmations help you maintain a grateful attitude. Through affirmations, you can clearly observe the multitude of good things in your life for which you have to show gratitude. Your ability to sense even subtle elements that bring immense joy is increased through affirmations.

- Affirmations enhance your positivity which directly impacts your confidence.

Try any of these confidence-building affirmations. Repeat them to yourself as often as you can. Do try to make some of your own as well:

- I am mindful, calm, and confident.

- I am happy with how I am today even as I will continue to improve myself.

- I have faith in my abilities and strengths to overcome obstacles.

- I have compassion towards myself and others.

- I am strong, wise, and powerful.

- I am complete by myself.

- My most important best friend is myself.

- I am thankful for this gift of life, and I will endeavor to live it meaningfully and purposefully.

- I have learned a lot by facing challenges.

- I am a unique woman, and this uniqueness is my individuality.

- I believe each day I get better than the previous day.

- I deserve my dreams because I can achieve them through hard work.

- I am confident that I can complete all my responsibilities satisfactorily.

- I am a positive woman, and I always look for the best in any given situation.

- I enjoy receiving compliments because I know I deserve them.

- I feel grateful for my life and all its offerings.

- I do not hesitate to give praise when I see good work.

- I am always in a learning state, and I find valuable lessons in a worst-case scenario.

- I have talents and I work hard to bring them to the fore.

- I am an enthusiastic worker and learner.

- I treat my mistakes as learning opportunities and quickly move on.

Every time you feel your level of confidence ebbing, sit in your favorite spot ensuring you will be undisturbed for a little while. Close your eyes and choose an affirmation that is aligned with your current situation. Repeat it in your mind for about 5 minutes even as you try to focus on the positive aspects of your life.

Affirmations are not magical and cannot drive away your problems. But they compel your entire being to work harmoniously thereby enhancing your chances of finding innovative solutions to life's myriad problems.

Visualization Techniques for Confidence

Oprah Winfrey, one of the most influential women of today, and one who has, perhaps, experienced and overcome all kinds of problems available in the world, says, *"You really can change your reality based on the way you think."*

Visualization can easily be referred to as 'daydreaming' but with a strong sense of purpose. Visualization helps to crystallize your visions and dreams. The famous beach volleyball duo, Kerri Walsh and Misty May-Treanor, use a lot of visualizations to achieve success. In their minds, they take in the smells, sounds, and cheers of victory even before getting down to the court to start their match. Arnold Schwarzenegger dreamed of having a body just like his role model, Reg Park. Jim Carrey visualized holding a cheque of 10 million dollars.

How does visualization work? Here's how. Suppose you imagine yourself alone and lonely with no one to love you and care for you. What happens to your body? Automatically, your body shrivels up, and your shoulders droop in sadness, right? In fact, if you think very deeply of sad situations, tears well up in your eyes unwittingly.

Similarly, think of a joyful situation. It could be a fun picnic day with your family where your children are frolicking on the beach and playing around in the water. You can hear their laughter and chatter in your mind. Automatically, your face lights up, and you can feel yourself smiling. These are direct experiences that nearly all of us have undergone.

Multiple research studies have revealed a strange phenomenon. It appears that when we imagine something in our head, then the brain cells in certain primal parts behave as if the imagined scene is actually taking place. Visualizations in our head are believed to impact the working of our central nervous system and drive our body to do what we are imagining to make it a reality.

Benefits of visualization - Here are some excellent benefits of visualization techniques:

- It compels your subconscious and unconscious minds to delve deep and find innovative solutions to achieve your dreams.

- It helps your brain to identify and attract people and resources needed to achieve your dreams.

- Continued practice of visualization techniques activates the law of attraction in your life bringing mentors, role models, necessary resources, and other things required to realize your dreams.

- It enhances your levels of confidence and motivation.

Here is a visualization template that you can use for any of your dreams.

Visualization exercise: Suppose you had to say no to your sister-in-law the next time she asks you to babysit her child while she is out partying with her friends. First, prepare what you will be saying to her. Make sure you have learned your prepared speech by rote. Next, sit comfortably in a quiet place, and visualize the following events:

- Imagine yourself giving that prepared speech confidently to your sister-in-law
- Imagine yourself speaking in a strong tone of voice firmly and confidently
- Imagine finding counterarguments for each of her arguments
- Visualize yourself confidently say, "No, I cannot help you this time."

Journal Writing for Confidence Building

William Wordsworth said this of journal writing, *"Fill your paper with the breathings of your heart."* There are multiple benefits related to confidence-building when you start and maintain a journal. Some of these benefits include:

- You have clarity on your goals and your progress which drives confidence; you see the daily, weekly, monthly progress of your goals, and feel confident about achieving the final goal; you can also make changes to your goals whenever needed
- Journaling helps in recovering from the effects of negative emotions
- Journaling shows you the inconsistencies in your life

helping you get rid of them

- Journaling improves your learning as you make notes of your daily experiences

- Journaling facilitates an attitude of gratitude.

You can also use journaling to convert your negative thoughts into positive ones. Here are some examples:

Negative thought: 'This is impossible to do.' To counter this negative thought, write detailed answers to the following questions:

- What are some of your biggest achievements to date?

- Can you think of a similar situation in your life when you thought it was impossible, and yet, you finished it successfully?

- What is the bravest thing you have done as of today?

Negative thought: 'I don't have enough knowledge and skills.' Answer the following questions with a lot of detail to counter this negative thought:

- What are the topics you are excellent in? What areas do you excel so much in that others come to you for help? What are the training programs and certifications you have attended?

- What are the things you can do to improve upon your present level of knowledge and skills?

Negative thought: 'I look so ugly and fat. I hate my body." Answer the following questions to prevent being overwhelmed by this negative thought:

59

- What are the best parts of your body? What are the elements for which you have received compliments from others?

- What are the things you should feel grateful for when it comes to your body? A pair of strong legs for dancing, skipping, and walking? A pair of strong arms to do your daily work without having to depend on someone else? A beautiful smile that lights up your face, and those of your children?

Negative thought: 'I have insufficient good qualities.' Your answers to the following questions will help you counter this negative thought, and drive it out of your system:

- What are the things you possess that you should be grateful for?

- What are the top two compliments you receive from people?

- What does your loving family think of you?

- What are the things you have earned on your own that you are proud of?

Negative thought: 'I am sure to fail, so why should I even try?' Answer the following to counter this:

- What are the great things that will happen if you DID NOT fail?

- What will be the worst scenario? What are the ways you can manage yourself and the situation even if this worst scenario were to take place?

Avoid Perfectionism

Obsession with perfectionism is a bane and not a boon. When you are obsessed with perfectionism, you feel demoralized and exhausting. When you strive for excellence, then you feel motivated. Remember that no one is perfect. That is why even pencils have erasers.

Giving your best efforts to all your endeavors is a healthy attitude. However, the obsession to get every teeny-weeny aspect of your activity perfect is dangerous and unhealthy. Perfectionists are plagued by self-doubt which, in turn, prevents them from trying a failed venture again. Thoughts of obsessed perfectionists go something like this:

- I hate myself the way I am; I wish I was better.
- I am not satisfied with how this has turned out even if my team and I have worked long, untiring hours on it.
- The world is black and white; things are either right or wrong
- If I become perfect, then I will be content and happy
- I am not achieving enough
- Efforts have no value if the results are less than perfect

Obsessed perfectionists face a lot of unnecessary challenges and waste their time and energy. Perfectionists, invariably, are lonely and unhappy

They are always anxious and tired – In their efforts to achieve perfection, they use up a lot of energy on small things that have little or no value. Therefore, perfectionists are always tired and anxious

They have unhappy relationships – They want only the best for themselves, and there are no best partners in the world. Therefore, all relationships of perfectionists are unhappy and unfulfilled. Whether it comes to spouses, parents, children or friends, perfectionists never seem to find fulfillment.

Here are some tips to overcome the obsession for perfection:

Know and accept that perfectionism is not absolute – What is perfect for you could be only a 'good enough' for someone, and what is 'good enough' for you could be 'perfect' for a different person. There is nothing like absolute perfectionism. The acceptance of this knowledge will prevent you from running after illusions.

Good enough is good too – 'Good enough' does not mean you don't try your best. It only means to let go and move on after you have given your best.

Know and acknowledge the imperfection in human beings – Humans are imperfect by nature. Our imperfections make us unique. Your fault is complemented by your spouse's fault thereby making your relationship workable.

For example, if you are a disciplinarian and your spouse is an easy-going person, then your children will have a normal childhood balanced beautifully by your discipline (when a situation calls for it) and his easygoing nature (when another kind of situation calls for it). If both of you were disciplinarians, your children's lives would be hell. Alternately, if both of you were easygoing, your children would never learn the value of discipline.

Most importantly, people who love and care for you will never reject you for not being perfect. Therefore, avoid perfectionism. Instead, focus on using your energies on building skills and your confidence levels.

Chapter Summary

This chapter discussed four different ways of building confidence including use of affirmations, use of visualization techniques, avoidance of perfectionism, and journal writing.

Chapter 7: Tips and Tricks to Build Confidence - Part II

Challenge Yourself Continuously

Challenging yourself, doing unfamiliar activities, accomplishing new tasks and projects, deliberately choosing a tough project, taking tough decisions, getting mentally and physically uncomfortable, and other similar kinds of activities are excellent ways of learning new things and building confidence. Also, helping others is a great confidence-booster. You must, of course, remember to equip and help yourself before you help others.

Every time you begin to feel comfortable in any place, you have lost the ability to learn anything new there. Challenge yourself continuously for learning and development. Whether it is at home or workplace, if you don't feel challenged by the work you do, then your confidence is stagnating. And stagnating is the beginning of a downfall.

Martin Luther King, Jr. said, *'The ultimate measure of a person is best gauged when he or she is passing through challenging and difficult times."* Therefore, be conscious about feeling challenged and avoid remaining in your comfort zone for long. Your level of complacency is directly proportional to the duration of your stay in comfort zones. Expand your skills in multiple domains because mastery over new skills can build your confidence significantly.

Raise your standards to get better at what you do. Here are some great tips to challenge yourself continuously:

Indulge in activities that you hate – If you hate to cook, make sure you cook at least three times a week. Don't worry excessively about how the food turns out. The challenge is in doing something you hate for a sustained period of time. If you don't like a particular colleague very much, seek her out, and start a conversation.

If you are uncomfortable dancing, join a class and learn dancing. Doing something you don't like is a fabulous way to remain challenged and out of your comfort zone. Your body and mind will resist your efforts, and you will need all your willpower to fight them; a great way to boost your confidence.

Live with your biggest fear or hate for a week – For example, if you hate traveling by public transport, use it for a week. If you hate to give speeches, make sure you give presentations in your office whenever there is an opportunity. If you don't like your mother-in-law, invite her to stay with you for a week.

You are likely to be benefited in two ways from this exercise: one is you will be challenging yourself throughout the week, and two is that it is very likely you will see how unfounded your fears and hate were. Both of these lessons are useful for boosting confidence.

Stay away from what you love the most for a week – If you love your daily dose of Netflix or other video streaming service, then uninstall the relevant app(s) for a week. If you enjoy being on social media, stay offline for a week. Again, there are two benefits possible. One is, of course, being challenged, and two is you could be able to get rid of a bad habit that was eating into your productivity.

Do things differently - Brush your teeth and eat your meals with your non-dominant hand. If you are a very talkative person, consciously refrain from talking. If you are a very silent person, then make an effort to talk more.

The intention of these tips is to move you out of your comfort zone and challenge yourself. When you feel uncomfortable, your body and mind are very alert which is a great setting to learn new things and build your confidence.

Love Yourself

If you don't love yourself, no one will be able to love you. Your relationship with yourself is the first step to building relationships with other people. Kim McMillen, the celebrated author of *'When I Loved Myself Enough,'* said, *"When I loved myself enough, I began leaving whatever wasn't healthy. This meant people, jobs, my own beliefs, and habits – anything that kept me small. My judgment called it disloyal. Now I see it as self-loving."*

Loving yourself does not call for selfishness or hating others or being narcissistic. On the contrary, loving yourself teaches you to be compassionate towards others too. Loving yourself only means that you are happy the way you are with all your strengths and weaknesses. Loving yourself only means you don't need external factors or people to make you feel complete and loved. Here are some fabulous benefits of self-love:

- When we love ourselves, we are okay with who we are, and our desire to be someone else disappears which, in turn, frees us from greed, resentment, and anger.
- We are free from anxiety about others' perceptions of us. We don't need to put up a façade anymore. Our life, behaviors, and actions are all authentic and aligned

with our inner real self.

- We don't feel lonely when we are alone because we love our own company.

- We don't need to depend on anyone to manage our weaknesses because we know we will always be there for ourselves.

- We become responsible for our happiness and take action towards achieving our goals without waiting for anyone else to help us.

Some great tips for self-love:

Be grateful for the good things in your life – When you are grateful for the good things in your life, you feel happy to have them. This happiness makes you love your life and yourself, leaving behind resentment for what you don't seem to have. Gratitude is the first step toward self-love.

Build a community of people who love you – Yes, external people may seem irrelevant while discussing self-love. Yet, people who love you and care for you increase your self-love. Build a community of such people around yourself.

Maintain a clutter-free and clean lifestyle – Eliminate all kinds of emotional, mental, and physical clutter from your life. Maintain a minimalistic, clean, and clutter-free lifestyle that is free from all kinds of negativity. This kind of clutter-free lifestyle will give you a great sense of freedom and lightness that makes you see yourself in a joyful and happy perspective thereby increasing self-love.

Stay away from negative people – Avoid all the people who demoralize and weaken you and make you feel unworthy. Such people's attitudes drive you to think of yourself as a useless person who doesn't deserve love. This attitude is counterproductive to increasing self-love. Therefore, stay away from negative-thinking people.

Have a Positive Attitude

Frances Hodgson Burnett, the British writer of three of the most famous and well-loved children's books (Little Lord Fauntleroy, The Secret Garden, and A Little Princess), said, *"If you look the right way, you can see that the whole world is a garden."*

Keeping a positive attitude attracts positive elements into your life. And the more positive elements in your life, the more your confidence will grow. Here are some amazing benefits to keeping a positive attitude:

High levels of motivation – A positive attitude keeps your mood levels on a positive note which means you feel motivated to work hard and give your best.

Challenges are seen as opportunities – Every obstacle and every challenge is seen as an opportunity to learn and grow. With a positive attitude, you will notice hidden opportunities even in your bleakest moment because you are filled with hope and motivation.

Reduced stress levels – Negativity and negative thoughts use up your energy resources for unproductive work such as managing stress and anxiety. A positive attitude allows you to focus on the good things in all elements thereby keeping anxiety at bay. Your energy resources are then freed up to be used for increased productivity and efficiency which, in turn, reduces stress levels again.

Here are some excellent tips to develop a positive attitude:

Live mindfully – Living mindfully requires you to be immersed in the present moment. When your entire being is fully engaged in experiencing the present moment, your body and mind are not riddled with past regrets or future worries. A life of mindfulness, therefore, keeps you 'in the moment' helping you to live life with fulfillment and a positive attitude.

Describe your life and yourself positively – Words have a powerful influence on our minds. If you choose to describe yourself as 'average,' 'boring,' 'uninteresting,' etc., your personality will reflect these emotions. Contrarily, when you describe yourself as a fun-loving, happy, and joyful woman, then the impact of these words get passed into your personality, and you will feel the happiness.

In the same way, use positive words to describe the work you do. If needed, sit down and make notes with the right choice of words to use when you are speaking to people about yourself, your job, or your life.

Be conscious of every action you take and every word you say and ensure they exude positivity. Think before you do or say anything so that you get time to choose positive over negative. Surround yourself with confident individuals so that you can learn from such people and imbibe their positive qualities.

Chapter Summary

In this chapter, you learned more ideas on how to build confidence including challenging yourself continuously, loving yourself, and having a positive attitude.

Conclusion

The main takeaways to build confidence include:

- Your decision to start being confident from today, and then every day

- Building your core values and imbibing them deeply into your psyche

- Using the core values to develop your life purpose and goals; breaking down the goals into daily, weekly, and monthly goals to keep track of them

- Building self-awareness to know your strengths and weaknesses

- Building confidence through various methods including loving yourself, maintaining a positive attitude, leveraging the power of affirmations and visualization techniques, and many more tips

- Living life on your terms by knowing your limits so that you are not negatively impacted by what others think of you

Increased confidence brings high levels of self-esteem and assertiveness into your life helping you to lead a more fulfilling and meaningful life than before. For more detailed information about self-esteem and assertiveness, refer to the following books:

- [Self-Esteem for Women](#)

- [Assertiveness for Women](#)

Part 2: Assertiveness for Women

Secret Tricks to Learn How to Say No Without Feeling Guilty and Get More Respect

Chapter 1: Introduction – Types of Communication

The best place to start learning about assertiveness is to know what communication is and the different types. So, what is communication? It is the exchange or passing of thoughts, ideas, and information between two or more people.

Communication facilitates meaningful interaction among human beings. It is the process through which human beings interact with and understand each other's thoughts, ideas, opinions, and emotions. Imagine what the world would be like if we could not communicate with each other! There are primarily four types of communication, including:

1. Passive communication
2. Aggressive communication
3. Passive-aggressive communication
4. Assertive communication

Therefore, assertiveness is a personality trait that is connected to communication. Assertive communication style is characterized by a woman's ability to express her thoughts, opinions, beliefs, and emotions firmly while ensuring she does not infringe on other people's freedom to express their thoughts, opinions, beliefs, and emotions.

Edith Eva Eger, the famous Hungarian-American writer, and a Holocaust survivor said, *"To be passive is to let others decide for you. To be aggressive is to decide for others. To be assertive is to decide for yourself. And to trust that there is enough, that you are enough."*

Assertiveness is the most preferred form because it is the most democratic style of communication. As an assertive woman, you will be able to say what you want to say and stand up for your rights without hurting people's feelings or subjugating other stakeholders' rights. A brief introduction to each of the four primary communication styles will help in improving your understanding of assertiveness.

Passive Communication

A woman with a passive communication style is one who does not stand up for her rights and beliefs. She will also not stand up for other people's rights and beliefs. A passive communicator is scared or does not have the willpower and mental strength to voice her thoughts, opinions, and emotions firmly and confidently.

As a passive communicator, even if you are hurt by other people's rude behavior or choice of words, you choose to remain silent instead of voicing your resentment. It is not that you don't want to raise your voice against injustice. You just can't find the power to do so.

A passive communicator is characterized by:

Shyness – Invariably, passive communicators are also shy, and find it difficult to speak confidently. For example, if your boss is loading you up with excessive work, then, because you are shy and don't want to attract attention to yourself, you will simply accept it instead of telling him or her that you cannot take on so much work.

Overly sensitive – Passive communicators are typically

excessively sensitive to criticism and take all feedback personally. So, for example, if your husband says that the food you cooked today is not very tasty, you will be hurt, and perhaps even start crying.

Deeply self-conscious – Ask yourself if you are overly worried about how you appear in front of other people. If the answer is yes, then it is an unmistakable sign of being a passive communicator. Such people are so worried about how they will be perceived by other people that they will not do anything that might make them unpopular.

The negativities from such instances accumulate in your system in the form of anxiety, stress, and feelings of inadequacy. Soon, these accumulated negativities will breach their threshold and find unpleasant and dangerous ways of release. Eleanor Roosevelt said, *"Nobody can make you feel inferior without your consent."* Therefore, it is up to each one of you to build the necessary skills to stand up for your rights, and stop being passive communicators.

Here are some classic responses and thoughts of a passive communicator:

- I am not very smart, and therefore, I cannot be more than a housewife.
- I am not worthy of love, and that is why no one will listen to me.
- I cannot dream of going out with that good-looking colleague because I am so ugly.
- My children and my family will never think highly of me.
- I am not worthy of becoming the branch manager; I

must simply be happy with my present low-level job status.

Challenges of a passive communicator:

- You will never be able to grow and develop yourself to your fullest potential.

- You will not be noticed for promotions even if you are skilled for the job.

- People will have unrealistic expectations from you, and whenever you fail to live up to these expectations, your self-belief will take a beating, resulting in low self-esteem.

- You are bound to feel that your life is not under your control.

- Your ability to mature and develop into a strong personality will be reduced considerably because your problem areas are rarely addressed.

- You are bound to suffer from depression and anxiety-related issues because of the accumulation of unnecessary negatives within your system.

Aggressive Communication

If passive communicators are at one end of the communication spectrum, passively giving in to other people's hurtful and insulting behavior, aggressive communicators are on the other end of the spectrum. They say what they want to say while violating the rights of others. Aggressive communicators are, most often, physically and/or verbally abusive.

Anne Campbell, the world-renowned British author and academic specializing in evolutionary psychology, says, *"Aggression is the first step on the slippery slope to selfishness and chaos."* People with an aggressive style of communication are characterized by:

An excessive focus on themselves – Aggressive communicators are almost always focused on themselves and have little or no regard for anyone else's views or opinions. The reason why such people choose to subjugate other people's thoughts and opinions is that they are focused on pursuing their personal agenda alone.

A woman with aggressive behavior wants only her messages and opinions to be heard, and all others' must be relegated forcefully to the background. Selfishness is one of the first attitudes that comes through in a woman behaving or communicating aggressively.

Complete lack of listening skills –Aggressive communicators' listening skills are pathetically low. Such people not only lack active listening skills but also do not have the basic listening skills needed to understand even the verbal part of the communication.

Aggressive communicators are focused only on presenting their own perspectives and viewpoints. Ironically, sometimes, they end up arguing even with those people who are actually agreeing with them! That is how poor their listening skills are.

Most often, during discussions involving an aggressive communicator, even if someone else manages to get across her viewpoint, her opinions will be rudely rejected for no rational reason.

A lack of empathy – Aggressive communicators have abysmal listening skills, and they are focused only on their personal goals. Both these attitudes are reflective of a personality that lacks empathy. Everyone else's emotions, thoughts, and pain are insignificant in the face of their selfishness.

These characteristic features of aggressive people make them appear violent, dominating, nasty, unpleasant, and insensitive.

Here are some classic responses and thoughts of an aggressive communicator:

- You are wrong, and I am right.
- I am better than you.
- I have no patience for you and your opinions.
- I must always get my way, by hook or by crook.
- I have every right to infringe upon your rights because I am superior to you.
- All the bad things happened because you did wrong, and all the right things happened because I did the right thing.

Challenges of an aggressive communicator:

- You will alienate friends, colleagues, and after some time, even family members and loved ones, and you will find yourself alone in this wide world, having no one left in your social, personal, and professional circle to show off your aggression to.
- Even if you have excellent oratory skills, you will not be

able to win any debates because you will not be invited.

- If you hold a position of power, you will be hated or feared; if you don't hold any position of power, you will be completely ignored. Either way, you will not find love or popularity.

- You will never grow and develop into a mature woman because real issues in your life are bound to remain unresolved.

Passive-Aggressive Communication

As the name suggests, this style of communication combines passive and aggressive styles. Women who are passive-aggressive hide their aggressive behavior behind a façade of passivity. Have you ever felt like murdering your boss for making you do a project you hate, but outwardly, you smile at her, and say, "Okay, I will do my best?" This behavior is a classic example of passive aggression.

You can commonly see passive-aggression in your children too, especially in their interactions and behaviors with seniors, elders, and other authority figures. For example, suppose you tell your teenage daughter to clean her room before she goes out partying with her friends. You come in after a few minutes, and you are quite likely to see the room cleaner than earlier. However, you will find everything that was lying around in the room now stuffed under the bed!

She may have passively listened to your command but she used a method where her aggression got its way too. If you try arguing with her, then the typical response will be, "You are always finding fault with me no matter what I do!" People with a passive-aggressive style of communication typically exhibit the following characteristics:

They use silent treatment very often – Sulking is one of the most common forms of passive-aggressive behavior seen in many women. Children sit grumpily, refusing to have dinner with everyone else at home, to show their displeasure.

They employ subtle insults – A colleague may appear as if she is giving you a compliment. However, if you think about it for a while, you will realize that it was a veiled insult.

They are quite vengeful – Their aggression is not entirely released from their system because they hide it well. Therefore, such people will not easily forgive and forget. They use subversive means to get revenge.

All these characteristics are noticeable by other people, and passive-aggressive communicators easily lose friends.

Here are some classic responses and thoughts of a passive-aggressive communicator:

- I am not angry (despite being very angry inside).
- Whatever! Fine!
- Wait, I am coming! (and taking more time than needed to come)
- You are always finding fault.

Challenges of passive-aggressive behavior

- Such people end up accumulating a lot of negativity within their system and becoming victims of depression and anxiety.
- Although they might release some of their negative

feelings through subversive means, the root problems remain unresolved.

- Once their true nature is revealed, such people also quickly alienate others.

Assertive Communication

This form of communication is what is most sought after by people. An assertive woman says what she wants to say and provides ample space for others to voice their viewpoints, thoughts, beliefs, and opinions. Assertive women are characterized by:

Respectful behavior – Assertive people value and respect everyone's viewpoint.

Self-belief and self-worth – Assertive people identify and acknowledge their strengths and weaknesses, and therefore, have a healthy level of self-belief and self-worth.

Sincere interaction – Assertive people don't believe in fluff. They make a sincere effort to participate in all their interactions with other people.

Excellent emotional quotient – Assertive people know how to manage their emotions, and exhibit excellent self-control even during heated arguments and discussions.

Great communication skills – Assertive people understand the importance of communication skills for accurately presenting their views and thoughts. Therefore, they work hard to build their communication skills.

Here are some classic responses and thoughts of an assertive communicator:

- I am right, and so are you. Let's find a common meeting ground.

- Everyone is entitled to their opinions and thoughts.

- I speak plainly and honestly.

- I value my personal rights, and I will ensure that I don't infringe on your individual rights.

Benefits of assertiveness – Being assertive has no challenges; only benefits. Let's look at some of them:

- You will earn the respect of everyone in your personal and professional circles.

- As you address the core issues of your personality and life, you will mature and develop as an individual, learning from your mistakes while accepting praise with humility.

- You will be popular and well-liked among your friends and colleagues.

- Being assertive gives you an excellent chance at leadership opportunities as most people will enjoy interacting and working for you.

Typically, men are seen as being more assertive than women. However, in modern times, this trend and perspective are changing rapidly. Many women have broken glass ceilings and have managed to become great leaders with their names deeply and inextricably etched in human history. Nearly all great women leaders have assertiveness as one of their most important and valuable traits. Building assertiveness is a critical skill in today's highly competitive environment.

Chapter 2: Why Do We Behave the Way We Do?

So, why are some of us aggressive, some of us passive-aggressive, and some of us assertive? Why do human beings behave the way we do? This chapter intends to provide some logical answers to this rather complex question.

When our ancestors were hunter-gatherers, the concept of civilization was yet unknown. Our ancestors behaved the way animals behave; exhibiting anger openly when they were angry, laughing out loud when something made them happy, crying when something made them sad, and so forth. Our ancestors lived literally from hand to mouth, eating well if they had a good hunt, and starving when they couldn't find food. They had no time or energy for anything but survival.

Gradually, human beings settled into the role of agriculturists and formed societies and civilizations. We had ample food and safe places to live, and our concerns about survival took a backseat. Now we had time for other things, and we began to look at ourselves and decided to change our behaviors to align with the changing times.

Along with many changes, we decided to change the way we expressed our emotions. We chose to categorize emotions into positive and negative. Happiness, joy, etc. were positive emotions, and anger, sadness, etc., were negative emotions. Slowly but surely, we trained ourselves to hide our negative emotions because it is considered "wrong" and "undignified" to cry during sadness or to show anger during upsetting times.

Unfortunately, human beings came to accept that suppressing emotions is the best way of handling them, and therefore, we trained ourselves and our children to hide our emotions and keep them inside. This training is one of the primary reasons why people behave the way they do.

Our emotions are not meant to be suppressed. Our emotions work in tandem with our intelligence to help us improve our understanding of the human world and its happenings. Emotions bring music to our lives. Yes, sometimes, the music might be sad. But, many times, emotions create happiness and beauty in our lives. And we need them for our sustenance.

Moreover, emotions are nothing but a form of energy. The excess emotional energy needs to be released or dissipated into the atmosphere to prevent unpleasantness. We can use the example of a coffee percolator to understand this situation. A coffee percolator is a machine that brews aromatic, delicious coffee. How does it work? Well, you add the coffee grounds and water and switch on the percolator.

The water will boil, and the grounds will release their strength into the water, resulting in wonderful coffee. The excess energy from the boiling water needs to be released, and should not be accumulated, lest the percolator burst and splash hot, burning coffee all over, wreaking havoc on your home.

Similarly, the emotional energy from our systems needs to be released and not accumulated. When we suppress our emotions, the energy gets accumulated and is counterproductive to a happy life. When the threshold of our ability to accumulate emotional energy is reached, it will burst forth in unpleasant and dangerous ways, resulting in chaos for everyone connected with such an individual.

Gwen-Randall Young, the famous award-winning psychologist, says, *"Aggression is different from anger. Anger is an emotion; aggression is a behavior. There are better ways to deal with anger than behaving aggressively. Aggressive talk, gestures, or behaviors belong to the old way of being. Once we tune in to a higher level of consciousness, aggression is as unnecessary as is the hand-held plow in modern-day agriculture."*

Expressing our emotions maturely and productively is the best form of releasing emotional energy. Suppressing emotions is an unhealthy way of handling emotions.

Reasons for Aggressive Behavior in Women

Before we go into the reasons for aggressive behavior in women in modern times, we need to understand gender differences when it comes to aggressive behavior. Even in the contemporary world, where gender differences are considerably less than what they were a couple of decades ago, men are still allowed to exhibit aggression far more than women.

Aggression is traditionally depicted as physical or verbal abuse that tends to hurt others. Typically, men are physically stronger than women. However, in today's modern world, aggression includes non-physical qualities such as excessive ambition, competitive spirit, and assertiveness bordering on an aggressive nature; all with the intention of achieving selfish ends.

Therefore, women are also quite aggressive today and do not hesitate to reflect the aggression in their behavior and attitude. Here are some reasons for aggressive behavior in women:

Childhood environment – Most often, aggressive behavior is learned during childhood. Parents who behave aggressively pass on these habits to their children, who observe and copy parental behavior. Therefore, if a child has seen a lot of fighting and abusive behavior between her parents, invariably, she will think that it is okay to behave like that and will pick up aggressive habits.

Unresolved problems of childhood – Girls who have had an abusive childhood in any form—physical, sexual, or emotional—whose issues have remained unresolved, typically display aggressive behavior in adulthood.

Stresses of the modern world – The woman of the modern world juggles too many things for her own good, and she wants to excel in everything she does. She wants to be a supermom. She wants to break the glass ceiling in the workplace. She wants to come across as a social animal who loves to party. Excessive self-expectations and societal expectations drive many women to behave aggressively as a way of coping with stress and unrealistic expectations. The modern woman wants to be perfect in everything she does; this is an unreasonable expectation that leads to excessive stress, and unwittingly, aggressive behavior.

Additionally, PMS and menopause result in fluctuating hormones, and childbirth complexities tend to increase the aggressive streak in women today. In fact, aggressive behavior is observed to increase after childbirth because of testosterone, a hormone directly connected to aggressive behavior. Testosterone levels in men are always higher than in women, and this is one of the primary reasons used to explain the aggression inherent in men more than women.

Here is an explanation that is given by medical experts for post-pregnancy aggression. During pregnancy, testosterone levels are low in women. After childbirth, testosterone levels rise, which could be a reason for increased aggressive behavior, post-delivery.

The desire to appear dominating – Men are traditionally considered more aggressive than women, and this reason is used many times to overlook women for promotions. Many women tend to use aggressive behavior to appear dominating so that they look capable of handling situations in the same way men do.

Low self-esteem – A woman suffering from low self-esteem uses aggression as a way to hide it from the outside world. She thinks that by showing aggressive behavior, people will think that she is strong and will not try to hurt her. Women with low self-esteem use aggressive behavior to mask their fears, insecurities, and frustrations about their own capabilities.

Reasons for Passive-Aggressive Behavior in Women

The primary difference between aggressive behavior and passive-aggressive behavior is the way the behavior is exhibited in the outside world. Women with an aggressive style of communication overtly use bad language or subjugate others' opinions and viewpoints. Passive-aggressive women behave passively but use aggressive behaviors subversively. Here are some reasons why some women choose passive-aggressive behavior over-aggressive behavior:

Aggressive behavior is socially unacceptable, especially for women – While everyone, irrespective of gender, is trained to hide their negative emotions and not show aggressive behavior, women, more than men, are expected to be "ladylike" and to refrain from "unruly" behavior.

These kinds of conventional ideas are deeply entrenched in

the minds of women from the time they are little girls. Therefore, many women prefer to hide their aggressive attitude behind a façade of passivity. They use subversive methods to get back at people who they believe have humiliated or insulted them. Therefore, it is common to find women colleagues carrying tales to their bosses about their coworkers while acting all nice and polite to their coworkers' faces.

Passive-aggressive behavior can be explained away easily – Muttering under one's breath, doing something wrong deliberately and then feigning an apology, etc., are easy to explain and get away with. It is very difficult to pinpoint such kinds of behaviors as wrong and pull up the people responsible for it.

For example, if you told your teenage daughter to study for her exam, she could pretend to study all night, and yet not do anything productive, right? She might be sitting at her desk with her book open, and her mind wandering somewhere else. How will you pull her up for this?

Revenge is sweet, indeed – Being vengeful is a typical trait of passive-aggressive people. They have not had the satisfaction of venting their aggressive feelings. So, they carry them around, looking for an opportune moment to get back at the person they are feeling vindictive against; because, after all, revenge is sweet.

A classic example; suppose you ask your daughter to peel the potatoes for you. There is a mound of potatoes, and she doesn't want to do the task. But she cannot openly say no, because she knows you are a strict disciplinarian. So, she will peel the potatoes in such a way that you might have to redo them! Shoddy work is a classic form of passive-aggressive behavior.

Jimmy Carter, the former US president, said, *"Aggression unopposed becomes a contagious disease."* So, heed his advice, and fight against any form of aggressive behavior you may have in your system. Instead, learn the skills of assertiveness, and get your work done nicely.

Chapter 3: Current Level of Assertiveness

Virginia Woolf said, *"Without self-awareness, we are as babies in the cradles."* Knowing yourself at a deep level is the first step to improving yourself. So, to improve your level of assertiveness, you should know where you are currently, and then make plans to move forward. This chapter, consisting of self-assessment questionnaires and quizzes, will help you gauge your current level of assertiveness. So, let's begin.

Questionnaire #1

Q1. Suppose you are waiting in line at a bank. There are people before you and after you. It is quite a long line. Now, someone walks into the bank, goes straight to the teller, and wants to be helped before the others waiting before him. Will you stand up and raise your voice against this person's actions? Y/N

Q2. You buy your husband a new cell phone for his birthday, and the salesman assures you that all the advertised features are available on the new phone. However, when your husband browses through the device, he finds a couple of features missing. Will you go back to the store (which is some distance away, and anyway, you got the phone at a huge discount) and demand an explanation or complain? Y/N

Q3. If you are angry with someone, for any reason whatsoever, do you typically express your feelings, backed by strong reasons for your anger? Y/N

Q4. You are helping your daughter with her school science project. You are a science major and know a lot about the subject. You have a big argument on the method to use for the project. Your daughter says the teacher wants it done one way, and you think it has to be done in a different way. In the end, you win the argument, and the work is completed your way. The next day, she takes the project to school and comes home with clear instructions from the teacher to redo the whole thing the same way that your daughter originally said it should be done. Will you apologize to your daughter and inform the teacher of your mistake? Y/N

Q5. If you are in a group discussion, do you make an effort to draw out people who don't appear comfortable talking or presenting their viewpoints? Y/N

Q6. Your elder sister, who has been your mentor until now, has been borrowing money from you frequently for the last couple of months. She gives some valid reasons for it. However, this time, she wants a relatively large amount, and you are concerned about her. Will you deny giving her the money and honestly explain your concerns? Y/N

Q7. If you are part of a group discussion, do you make an effort to express your viewpoints strongly? Y/N

Q8. Your new, hot neighbor has finally asked you out on a date to one of your favorite restaurants in town. You are thrilled and want to make sure nothing goes wrong. Your orders arrive, and you notice that the dish you ordered is not really what you asked for. Even at the risk of appearing unduly finicky in front of your date, will you call the waiter and ask him to get you a correctly-done order? Y/N

Q9. Do you feel comfortable asking for favors, including requests for financial help, from your friends and family? Y/N

Q10. Your son is studying for an important upcoming exam. A big group of your friends unexpectedly comes over, wanting to spend the day at your house. The noise is sure to disturb your son's study. Will you politely tell your friends to come back another day? Y/N

Q11. You have been saving money to buy that charming ruby necklace you have been eyeing at the new jewelry store. Finally, you have the money, and visit the store to pick it up. The salesgirl at the counter shows you a pair of gorgeous matching ruby earrings to go with the necklace. The addition of the pair of earrings will cost you more than you budgeted for. Will you be able to firmly say no? Y/N

Q12. Are you comfortable talking about your opinions, including sensitive matters, with your close family and friends? Y/N

Q13. Are you comfortable airing your viewpoints on sensitive matters with your colleagues? Y/N

Q14. Your old mentor is giving a presentation at your office. Suddenly, you notice she or he says something incorrectly, which could mislead everyone present. Will you stand up and correct your mentor? Y/N

Q15. You go to the local grocery store, pick up the groceries, and after paying, you take the change from the clerk without counting it and leave the store. When you get home, you find that you were short-changed. Will you go back to the store and ask for the difference? Y/N

Q16. A relative whom you think very highly of, and who has taught you things that have helped you achieve success, comes home to visit for the first time in years. She has become old and sad. Her views have undergone huge changes (for the worse), and you are startled at the change. She says something that you disagree with strongly. In fact, it's the opposite of an idea you once learned from her. Will you express your disagreement? Y/N

Q17. An old school friend is going through a bad patch in her life. She has helped you many times in the past by lending you money. You have returned all the money owed to her. However, she still holds an important place in your heart because she helped you when you needed her the most. Now she comes to you with a request that is not just unreasonable but also illegal. Your friend says this is what she wants in return for the goodwill you have for her. Will you stand up and tell her no? Y/N

Q18. Your children and the neighbors' kids are trying to earn a place on the school's quiz team. There is a written quiz for the qualifying round and more than fifty students are vying for the four places. By some stroke of luck, your neighbor's children figure out the questions that are likely to be asked during the qualifying round. Your neighbor shares those questions with you so that your children and hers can both have an advantage. Will you raise your voice against this injustice and let the school know so that they can change the questions? Y/N

Q19. Your parents are going through a rough divorce, and your mother wants to come and live with you for a few months. Your house is already quite full, and you really cannot accommodate her even for a few months. Will you tell her so politely but firmly? Y/N

Q20. You and your boyfriend of many years have decided to get married, and the date is set. He is really well-to-do, and marrying him will give you a life of comfort. Thinking that he now deserves to know all about you, you tell him a couple of little-known (and embarrassing) secrets about yourself, including one that involves a dear and close friend. However, your fiancé goes around revealing this information to everyone. Will you concede that you didn't really know your boyfriend well, speak out against his betrayal, and leave him? Y/N

Q21. You and a couple of other people are patiently waiting for your turn to be helped by the lone billing clerk in a department store. A young girl walks past the line, gives the clerk an enticing look, and gets helped before all of you. Will you complain about this behavior? Y/N

Q22. One of your colleagues borrows money from you and promises to return it within a month. However, now it has been nearly two months, and there is no sign of him returning the borrowed amount. Will you approach him directly and ask for the money back? Y/N

Q23. You usually don't have a problem laughing at yourself. However, one particular day, a colleague repeatedly mocks you despite you telling him politely (and discreetly) that he is crossing the line. Will you stand up and tell him so in front of other colleagues? Y/N

Q24. You arrive late for your child's school play. She is one of the main characters in it, so you have been given a seat right in front. Will you walk right up and take your seat, knowing that everyone will see you came in late? There are vacant seats at the back that you can occupy unobtrusively. Y/N

Q25. You are discussing something personal but important with your team members. She is sharing a personal problem with you. Halfway through the discussion, your boss walks in and wants to talk about an upcoming project. Will you politely tell your boss to give you a few minutes to complete the conversation with your team members? Y/N

Questionnaire #2

Choose the most appropriate response to know what style of communication you typically use:

Q1. You are waiting in line for the bus, and someone rudely cuts in line. What will be your response?

1. Gently show the person that there is a line to be followed.
2. Give him glaring looks and "accidentally" shove him back.
3. Firmly tell the man to join his rightful place in the line.
4. Say or do nothing.

Q2. Your cousin is supposed to be coming over to your house at nine a.m. to learn a new recipe. However, she only arrives at ten. What do you do?

1. Rudely tell your cousin you don't like to be kept waiting.
2. Don't say anything, and pretend nothing has happened.
3. Ask her for a reason for her delay, and tell her not to repeat this behavior.
4. Leave the house at 9:30 so she finds it empty when she arrives.

Journaling to Gauge Your Current Level of Assertiveness

For about a month, note down details of your daily experiences. Keep track of the following points while you make entries in your journal:

- Did you state your viewpoints confidently?
- What was your communication style?
- What were your emotions?
- Do you think you managed your feelings maturely?
- Was the result of the event affected by your emotions?
- How could you have handled the situation in a better way?

When you are writing down your experiences, remember not to judge yourself. Be objective, and make copious notes of everything.

Use all three templates given in this chapter to gauge your current level of assertiveness. Make your plans to move forward from here on. Maya Angelou, one of the most brilliant women writers of modern times, said, *"When you know better, you do better."*

Chapter 4: Building Assertiveness Based On Your Core Values

Patrick Lencioni, the American writer famous for his books on business management, says, *"A core value is something that you are willing to be punished for."* Before you identify your core values, let us look at the definition of core values, and their importance in our lives.

So, what are the core values? They are those qualities or personal traits that act like compasses, showing us the path to our personal goals. Core values enhance the value of your achievements and guide you through your life's path. In the absence of core values, we merely drift along, going wherever external circumstances and other people choose to take us.

The absence of core values means you are leading a directionless life. It means your life is not your own. It belongs to the person(s) who is/are leading you along. Yolanda Hadid, a popular reality TV star, says, *"I understand that my soul is my power; not my ego or perfection. If we can maintain our core values, which describe our soul, authentically, then the exteriors take second place. We find purpose in our lives."*

Importance of Core Values

Core values give our lives a sense of purpose – Core values help us make life choices that are aligned with our needs and requirements. For example, suppose family love is one of your core values, and it comes above career. Now, take an example when you have to choose between working on a weekend, because of an upcoming project, and taking your children out on a weekend picnic.

With a core value of family love being more important than career, you will easily pick taking your kids out for a weekend picnic over going to the office. That particular core value of family love gives you a sense of purpose. You purposefully choose one thing over another because you are driven by your core values.

Core values simplify our decision-making processes – Take the above example again. It is so easy to choose your kids' overwork because your core values are deeply entrenched in your psyche. You don't need to deliberate excessively. Look at the choices you have, see which of them are aligned with your core values, and choose accordingly. Thus, core values simplify our decision-making processes.

Core values enhance our confidence – Core values are powerful life-skill tools that give us a sense of purpose and help us lead an authentic life, driven by our souls. In such circumstances, failures and successes don't define our confidence. Living life meaningfully defines confidence, and that's what core values help us with; to live life from the depths of our souls.

Identifying Your Core Values

There are hundreds of core values from which you can choose those that best suit your lifestyle. However, instead of choosing from a predesignated list, you can discover your core values from your own experiences because core values are inherent in our personality, and all we need to do is discover, identify, and label them. Use the following template to delve deep within your soul and write your answers to the different self-assessment questions.

Recall the top-five best and happiest experiences in

your life – Remember those events, and answer the following questions for each of the experiences:

Describe in detail what happened. When? What? How? Who were the other people present?

_____

What were your feelings at that time?

_____

What were your thoughts?

_____

What were the core values that were clearly displayed during those experiences? If the event happened when you were very little, you may not have known what core values were part of the experience. However, now, reliving those experiences, you will clearly see the core values standing out.

_____

Don't worry about recalling events in great detail. Just close your eyes and let your mind wander. Many of our beautiful memories are deeply etched in our minds, and when we consciously reach out to them, most of the images come forth with little or no effort. So, go ahead, give in to this self-assessment exercise, and find the answers to the questions asked.

Recall the worst or saddest five experiences of your life – Again, write down your answers to the same set of questions as above. However, the last question will be reworded as, "What are the core values that you believe were suppressed in these experiences?"

Describe in detail what happened. When? What? How? Who were the other people present?

_____

What were your feelings at that time?

_____

What were your thoughts?

_____

What are the core values that you believe were suppressed in these experiences?

_____

Next, figure out your code of conduct – Your code of conduct will be driven by those elements that make your life meaningful. After your basic survival needs are taken care of, what are the things you need to live a fulfilling life? What are the elements without which your life will feel empty and barren? You will never thrive without these items. Here are a few examples to help you understand better:

- Adventure and travel
- Learning
- Family happiness
- Career progression
- Nature
- Health and vitality
- Financial security

Write down the list of all the core values you collected – From the above three exercises, you will have acquired a fairly big list of core values. Put them all together on a piece of paper.

Combine similar values together – It is highly likely that you will have acquired a rather long list of core values. Use the list to combine similar values together. For example:

- Discipline, timeliness, dedication, commitment, etc. can be one group.

- Prayers, spirituality, wisdom, godliness, faith, etc. can also be grouped together.

Label the central theme of each group – In the above examples, discipline timeliness, dedication, and commitment can be labeled as "discipline." Prayers, spirituality, wisdom, godliness, and faith can be labeled as "faith in the divine" or "spirituality."

Create your final list of core values – From this list, take the top five to ten items. They will become your unique and personal core values. The number range five to ten is important because a list with less than five elements might not cover all life aspects, and a list with over ten elements might be so cumbersome to keep track of that it will dilute the entire exercise of creating core values for a meaningful and fulfilling life.

Rank your list of core values – Prioritize your core values based on their importance in your life. This exercise might take longer than you think because ranking a list of items, all of which appear equally important, is a big challenge. So, how do you decide which is more important than others? Here is a tip.

Recall your best and worst experiences again, and this time, focus on the intensity of the emotions you felt. The higher the intensity, the more important the emotion and the corresponding core value. The ranking is an important activity in completing an effective core value list. You will need the ranking in those situations when two or more of your core values are in conflict with each other and you feel compelled to choose one over the other.

Using Your Core Values to Enhance Your Assertiveness

Once you get your core values deeply ingrained in your psyche, you will notice that it becomes easier than before to be assertive and stand up for your beliefs and principles. The resolute clarity on your core values gives you this power. Moreover, assertiveness goes beyond being a form of communication style. Assertiveness includes other aspects of life, including:

Keeping our promises – Being assertive includes being self-assertive which, in turn, calls for keeping promises you make. Core values help you keep your promises because they prevent you from straying from your life's purpose.

Keeps us from having to second-guess our choices – Assertiveness includes our ability to take responsibility for our choices and not second-guess our decisions. Core values help us make clear decisions that are aligned with our life's purpose, thereby ensuring we do not need to second-guess our choices.

Keeping our commitment to our life goals – Our goals in life are nothing but our promises to ourselves. Therefore, similar to keeping promises made to other people, core values help us keep our promises to ourselves. This attitude, in turn, helps us say no to counterproductive elements that can hinder our growth and development.

Thus, discovering, identifying, and labeling your core values is, perhaps, the first and the most important step to increasing your level of assertiveness.

Chapter 5: Change Your Inner Beliefs

One of the biggest hindrances to building our assertiveness is our inner belief. As we grow and develop in human society, interacting with each other, we are taught certain things, and we think that we should live only by these beliefs.

These inner beliefs are deeply embedded in our psyche and prevent us from effecting positive changes in our lives. For example, as children, we are taught that we must not show anger because it is wrong for kids to be angry. At the time, it might make sense, because kids invariably use tantrums to show their anger. Therefore, to tell them that showing anger is unacceptable is an effective way to bring about discipline in children and to teach them the importance of managing negative emotions.

However, if this outdated lesson remains in your psyche even as a grown woman, and you simply continue to suppress negative emotions such as anger and sadness, then the coffee percolator effect is bound to negatively impact your life. Therefore, these kinds of irrelevant and valueless inner beliefs should be removed from your mindset, and replaced with relevant and sensible beliefs. Here are some inner beliefs that promote unassertive thinking and prevent us from building assertiveness:

- I should not talk about my negative emotions because it is not right to burden others with my problems.
- Asserting my opinions and thoughts might make the other person feel bad, which could ruin my good relationship with him or her.

- It is embarrassing to openly talk about feelings and emotions because they are private and meant to be hidden.

- If my friend refuses to help me once, then it means he or she doesn't like me.

- People who care about me should be able to read my thoughts, and people who don't care about me shouldn't know my thoughts. Therefore, I shouldn't be talking about my emotions.

- Saying everything I want to say is selfish.

- No one, including me, can change their minds.

- Typically, emotions should be hidden inside a person's mind.

- If I talk about fear and nervousness, then I will be seen as weak which could make people mock me.

- Accepting praise is a sign of arrogance.

In 1975, Manuel J. Smith wrote a book titled, *When I Say No, I Feel Guilty*. In that book, he proposed a "bill of assertive rights" which he believed every human being should have. The "bill of assertive rights" is a collection of inner beliefs and thoughts that promote assertiveness. Some of them include:

- Everyone, including me, has a right to be the judge of his or her own behavior, thoughts, and emotions, and to accept responsibility for their consequences.

- Everyone has a right to say no.

- There is no need to justify your actions or behavior.

- You get the power to judge other people's behavior or actions only if you take the responsibility of finding solutions to their problems.

- Everyone has the right to change his or her mind.

- Everyone has the right to choose to agree or disagree with other people's opinions.

- Everyone has the right to commit errors and to take responsibility for the consequences of those errors.

- Everyone has the right to say, "I don't know," or "I don't understand," or "I don't care."

- Everyone has the right to make illogical choices and decisions.

Changing Your Inner Beliefs

Kilroy J. Oldster, the famous trial attorney, mediator, and arbitrator, and the author of Dead Toad Scrolls says, "Life has a tendency to provide a person with what they need in order to grow. Our beliefs, what we value in life, provide the roadmap for the type of life that we experience. A period of personal unhappiness reveals that our values are misplaced and we are on the wrong path. Unless a person changes their values and ideas, they will continue to experience discontentment."

So, to become more assertiveness than before, you must change your inner beliefs from those that promote unassertive thinking to those that promote assertive thinking. Some of us can change our inner beliefs by simply knowing and accepting that they have to be changed for our own good.

However, many of us don't have the luxury of having such a

flexible mindset. We need to find reasons and evidence as to why the old inner beliefs don't make sense, and how the new inner belief will help us grow and develop our assertiveness skills. Psychologists call this approach to challenging old inner beliefs head-on, in order to change them, "disputation."

The process of disputation is based on the idea that all our inner beliefs are not facts but learned opinions. While facts cannot be changed, opinions can be easily altered to suit a particular situation. Harmful opinions need not be blindly followed. We can dispute and counter these opinions, and create new and more valuable ones than before. Thought diaries are an effective means of tracking inner beliefs and raising suitable disputes to counter them.

Maintaining thought diaries – Our thoughts are not just random but nebulous and get lost somewhere in the depths of our mind while leaving behind the emotions. Human beings have no problem handling positive emotions triggered by positive thoughts. However, we are left scrambling for cover when there is a barrage of negative emotions triggered by negative thoughts. Maintaining thought diaries is the best way to manage these random, nebulous, and highly erratic thoughts.

Let us take an illustration to help you understand how to maintain thought diaries to counter old inner beliefs. Suppose you ask a good friend to help you with some money to tide you over during a particularly bad phase in your life. She rudely says no. You are taken aback by her reaction because you believed she would help you, as you helped her earlier in the same way, So, why didn't she? Now, this is the situation we have to write our thought diary. The thought diary has two parts:

Part I requires you to write about your emotions, thoughts,

and behavior.

Part II requires you to delve deep within your mind to find evidence for or against your thoughts and emotions.

Part I - Identifying your emotions – Find answers to the following questions:

What were your emotions? In addition to identifying your emotions, you must also rate them from 1 to 10; 1 being least intense and 10 being most intense. For example, if you felt anger and the intensity rating you give is 8, then it means your anger was quite intense.

Part I - Identifying your thoughts – Find answers to the following questions:

What were your thoughts? Were you asking yourself why your friend behaved the way she did? Or were you worried that maybe she was getting back at you for something you did that hurt her? Again, rate the intensity of your thoughts from 1 to 10.

Part I – Identifying your behavior – Find answers to the following questions:

What did you do? Did you say something nasty to her? Or did you ignore her calls? Also, what were your physical sensations? Rate the intensity of your behavior from 1 to 10.

Follow the rule of sticking to facts while making entries in your thought diary. Do not include your opinions and interpretations. Write down only facts. For example, "My friend refused to help me with money today," is factual, whereas "My friend rudely pushed me away when I asked for money that I needed desperately," reeks of your opinion and interpretation.

Part II – Answer the following questions honestly:

What kind of communication style did I employ in this entire situation? Was it aggressive, passive, or anything else? What kind of evidence is there for this behavior?

_____

Is there any evidence or proof that drove affected my emotions, thoughts, and behaviors?

_____

Was I making sure that both my and my friend's assertive rights were being upheld?

_____

Was I missing any element while I was undergoing the effects of my thoughts, emotions, and behaviors?

_____

How could I have improved on my behavior?

_____

Here are some illustrative examples for the answers that you might come up with when you reflect on the given situation:

Part I

What were your emotions? *I was angry and hurt by her*

refusal. Intensity of the emotion: 8

What were your thoughts? *I was thinking, "I have helped her so many times before. She should do the same for me now." Intensity: 8*

What did you do? *When she called me after this refusal, I did not pick up her call. She called me three times, and I ignored her call all three times. I did not call her back. Intensity: 8*

Part II

What kind of communication style did I employ in this entire situation? *I was behaving in a passive-aggressive manner by not telling her about my hurt feelings in an open way, and instead, choosing to ignore her calls.*

Is there any evidence or proof that drove affected my emotions, thoughts, and behaviors? *No, there is no evidence at all. These are only my feelings and opinions*

Was I making sure that both my and my friend's assertive rights were being upheld? *No, one of the first assertive rights that I was ignoring was that everyone has a right to say no.*

Was I missing any element while I was undergoing the effects of my thoughts, emotions, and behaviors? *Yes, there have been multiple times in the past when my friend has come to my rescue. Maybe there was a really compelling reason for her to have said no to me this time.*

How could I have improved my behavior? *I could have been more upfront, and asked her the reason for her refusal. I could have asked if she has some problems that I could help solve because her behavior was not really normal.*

After you have read your observations in Part II, try and rate the intensity of your emotions and thoughts, and you will notice that there is a considerable decrease. Therefore, using thought diaries, you can dispute your old inner beliefs and replace them with relevant and useful ones. Moreover, thought diaries help you look at your emotions with increased objectivity which, in turn, will help you manage situations more productively than before.

Chapter 6: Communication Techniques to Practice

To begin making positive changes in your communication techniques, you must first know what reasons drive people to use one or more of the four primary communication styles discussed in Chapter 1. Miranda Kerr, the famous Australian model, says, *"If you have the knowledge of how to take care of yourself, you can be a better version of yourself."*

Reasons Driving Passive Communication

- Wanting to please everyone around
- Lack of self-confidence
- Excessively worrying about whether expressed opinions will be taken the right way or not
- Excessively sensitive to criticism
- Lack of assertiveness

Reasons Driving Aggressive Communication

- Excessively focusing on achieving one's own ends with little or no empathy

- Wanting to please only oneself
- Overconfidence
- Utter disregard for others' viewpoints and opinions
- Poor listening skills

Reasons Driving Assertive Communication

- High level of confidence with no arrogance
- High level of self-awareness regarding both strengths and weaknesses
- Self-acceptance
- High level of resilience to criticism and feedback
- Always in learning mode

Here are some excellent tips and techniques that will help you improve your communication techniques for increased assertiveness.

Build Listening Skills

One of the biggest hurdles to improving assertiveness is a lack of listening skills. Most people resorting to aggressive or passive forms of communication and behavior do not have the ability to listen to what is being said in the right spirit.

Assertiveness calls for outstanding listening skills because that is what helps you discern between valuable and valueless thoughts and ideas; both your own and those of others. This discerning power allows you to make sensible assertive statements that can be accepted by all. Here are some tips to build listening skills:

Be present in the conversation – It is not just about being physically present. Your physical body, thoughts, heart, mind, and your entire being must be focused on the conversation that is taking place. Get rid of distractive elements such as your electronic devices while talking to people. Maintain healthy eye contact with the person(s) involved in the conversation so that they know that you are listening to them.

Focus on the speaker without appearing dominating or overbearing. This tip is especially important because, many times, in our earnestness to be "good listeners," we end up putting on an act of focusing excessively on the speaker which can be uncomfortable for other people.

Don't be judgmental – Everyone has a right to his or her opinion. This is one of the most important elements in the "bill of assertive rights" that was discussed in Chapter 5. Therefore, as a listener, you do not have the right to judge other people's views and opinions. Listen with an open and objective mind.

Listening without being judgmental allows you to hear viewpoints without mockery or malice. It allows you to simply respect that every opinion has something good in it. This objective perspective ensures you get the advantage of using the value in every viewpoint and idea.

Don't interrupt the speaker in the middle – When someone is talking, don't interrupt him or her to impose your solutions. It is possible that you can see a perspective relevant to the point that the speaker is talking about. He or she might have missed the point. Even in such scenarios, you must not interrupt the speaker in the middle.

Wait for the person to finish what he has to say, and then put forth your viewpoint. Abruptly interrupting a speaker sends multiple wrong messages, including:

- I don't want to listen to your ideas.
- My opinion is better (or more important) than yours.
- You are wasting my time.
- I don't care about your ideas.

All these messages, underlying your rude interruptions, are reflective of aggression. Therefore, to reduce aggression and improve assertiveness, avoid interrupting a speaker.

Identify Your Assertive Tone of Voice

In the movie *The Devil Wears Prada*, Meryl Streep speaks assertively throughout the film. She doesn't need to raise her voice to get people to obey her commands. She simply says her lines in a matter-of-fact tone that reeks of assertiveness. That is the kind of tone of voice you must identify for yourself.

Here are some tips to identify the natural tone of voice that you use in ordinary circumstances, such as asking someone at the dinner table to "pass the salt." That is the tone of voice you must identify and use in all your conversations in order to be more assertive than before. Follow these steps to identify your "pass the salt" voice:

Step #1 – Identify your natural tone of voice. For this, focus on how you say ordinary things to people. For example, if you are sitting at the dinner table, and you ask someone (anyone at the table) to pass the salt, what is your tone of voice? Focus on this tone, and learn to recognize it.

This is the most natural tone for you, and this tone is what you must use in all situations to improve your assertiveness. This natural tone of voice comes without any emotion or judgment and reflects assertiveness in the best way possible. Remember, this natural tone of voice does not hurt anyone; a key element for assertiveness.

Step #2 – Identify all the situations in your life when your tone of voice sounds "off," too loud, or too soft, driven by uncontrollable emotions. Recall these experiences and write them down. Here are some prompts to help you get started:

- What is your comfort level at a business/workplace meeting?
- How comfortable do you feel when sharing your thoughts and opinions when your bosses are present, when only your teammates are there, and when both are there?
- Do you believe your colleagues are positive when you talk at a meeting?
- How comfortable are you when talking to your loved ones and close friends (the ones you are fond of)?
- How comfortable are you when speaking to people you are not fond of?
- What is your comfort level when talking to strangers on the road whom you know you will not meet again?

Use these prompts to identify altered-voice situations. For example, if you are comfortable in an office meeting when your boss is present, what kind of voice do you use? Is it very soft, shrill, or something else? Or is it normal? In the same way, identify your tone of voice for each of the above prompts, and write it down. From these notes, you will be able to see where you are assertive and where you are not.

Step #3 – Pick out all those situations where you are not using the "pass-the-salt" voice. Typically, it means you are uncomfortable in these situations. Now, practice each of the awkward situations using your natural tone of voice. Initially, you are going to find it weird to use a natural tone of voice in situations that are emotionally charged with anger, sadness, happiness, etc.

However, don't give up. Keep practicing by saying emotion-laden and uncomfortable sentences in your normal tone of voice. With patient practice, you will realize that you can say things without raising your voice, and yet come across as assertive and firm.

Step #4 – After you have achieved a comfort level by practicing alone, use your efforts into the real-world as well. Use this normal tone of voice when you are angry with your child or spouse or someone whom you trust. They will notice the difference, and you will see whether your efforts are bearing fruit.

Alternately, practice the voice when you are talking to strangers or salespeople. For example, suppose you notice a particular salesgirl is trying to sell you something you don't want. You can feel your irritation rising. Be conscious of this emotion. Put it aside, and then deliberately use your natural tone of voice to say no to the pestering salesgirl.

In this manner, slowly practice using your "pass the salt" tone of voice in real-world situations. With some effort, you will notice that your discomfort with handling difficult situations will be considerably reduced, and your assertiveness will get a huge boost.

Learn to Say No and Use Assertive Phrases and Words

Learning to say no more often will help you make only those promises you can keep; a crucial element for assertiveness. Here are some commonly used "saying no" phrases that work in many situations. Learn them, practice them, and use them when needed:

- Thank you for offering me this opportunity; however, I am a bit tied up right now.

- Thanks for including me but I am afraid I have to pass up the offer this time.

- Thank you for reaching out to me; however, I have to say no now because I am busy with some other important work.

- This sounds like a good plan. Can I review it and get back to you in a couple of weeks?

- Thanks a lot for your opinion. Who are the other people in the group? Does anyone have a different idea?

- I disagree with you; however, you are entitled to your opinion.

- You are free to disagree with me. However, you cannot humiliate me or insult me for my views.

- I am offended by your tone of voice (or behavior or choice of words).

Learn to Handle Criticism Effectively

Assertive people handle criticism in the right spirit. They take constructive criticism seriously, but not personally, for self-improvement. They take unwarranted criticism by simply letting it go. Barbra Streisand's mother said of her daughter (long before her daughter became an icon in the film and music industry), *"She cannot be a good singer because her voice is not good, and she can't be a great actress because she is not beautiful."* We all know today how wrong this criticism was.

Barbra Streisand knew it was wrong even as a child. Instead of taking her mother's words personally, she chose to build her singing and acting skills. Like Barbra Streisand, develop your criticism-handling skills to get better at assertiveness and improve your self-learning.

Criticisms are primarily of three types, including:

1. Criticism because of a genuine mistake
2. Constructive criticism was given by well-wishers
3. Valueless and unfounded criticism

Let's look at how we can handle each of these:

Criticism because of a genuine mistake – We are all human beings, and being imperfect is natural to us. We all make mistakes, and if someone points out a genuine mistake, then you must accept it humbly, and thank the person for taking the trouble of pointing it out to you. Of course, after that, you must try and correct the mistake. This can be a great way of improving self-learning and getting better at your skills.

Constructive criticism was given by well-wishers –

Most well-wishers want only the best to happen to us. These people will leave no stone unturned (including giving you some seemingly harsh feedback) to help you achieve your potential.

Criticism from well-wishers is typically constructive in nature. It is imperative that you see them for their real worth, and apply them for self-improvement and personal development. It would be foolhardy to ignore or disregard well-meant criticism from everyone, especially those who care for you.

Valueless and unfounded criticism – In the midst of all the nice people in your life, you will find those who enjoy squirming at your discomfort. Such people's criticism is typically meant to hurt or dissuade you from trying harder and getting better. It is best to ignore such forms of criticisms.

Remember Ralph Waldo Emerson's words*: "Let me never fall into the vulgar mistake of dreaming that I am persecuted whenever I am contradicted."* Take criticism in the right spirit and work on improving yourself.

Chapter 7: Tools to Build Assertiveness

Your body language and posture speak volumes about your communication style. It is possible to gauge a person's confidence and assertiveness level by the way she sits, stands, and gesticulates. For example, a passive woman will typically hunch her shoulders and sit with her head down; a symbol of uncertainty and fear. However, an assertive and confident lady will keep her shoulders straight and look into the speaker's eyes during any interaction.

Nonverbal cues, including body language, play a very important part in your communication technique. A keen observer will be able to quickly discern the more powerful team at a meeting merely by watching people's body language. Body language cues are universal and cut across geographical and cultural barriers. For example, a smile is a sign of happiness irrespective of whether you are from Africa, America, Asia, or even remote Antarctica.

Interestingly, the animal kingdom (other than humans) also uses body language to communicate. For instance, gorillas and apes expand their chest as a form of dominance over other animals. That is to say, animals present an "opening up" gesture in the form of spreading out their arms and wings to exhibit dominance and aggression.

In the same way, human beings use this "expansive" gesture to suggest dominance. Here is a classic example. Have you seen runners (especially the winners of a race) cross the finish line with their arms spread out and high above their heads, and their heads held high? That is an expansive gesture reflecting their dominance and power in that race. Watch the ones who come last in the race. You will notice their hands are hanging down at their sides, and their faces are looking down to the ground.

Similarly, have you noticed two people, belonging to different hierarchies of power, standing next to each other? Well, if you take a moment to notice it, you will realize that the two individuals complement each other's body language. For example, if you are standing next to your boss, it is very likely that your boss is standing with his hands on his (or her) hips while you are standing with your hands at your sides or clasped together in front of you; one expansive and the other subdued.

Likewise, next time, watch your boss and his boss and notice how they look when they stand next to each other. Your boss will invariably take on your posture (hands down at the sides or clasped in front), and your boss' boss will have his or her hands on his or her hips! This is a natural stance taken by human beings (and animals) who feel unequal to each other.

Power Pose for Increased Assertiveness

Multiple scientific studies have revealed that confidence and assertiveness are connected to two particular hormones: testosterone and cortisol. Testosterone is believed to be related to confidence, and cortisol is related to anxiety and stress as follows:

- The higher the level of testosterone, the higher the level of confidence
- The lower the level of cortisol, the lower the level of stress and anxiety

This relationship between testosterone and confidence, and cortisol and anxiety is found in both men and women. Therefore, your confidence and assertiveness get a boost when testosterone levels are high and cortisol levels are low. Thus, balancing the levels of these two critical hormones in your body can have a direct impact on assertiveness.

The "power pose" is one of those postures that is believed to balance the levels of these two hormones in such a way that assertiveness and confidence are increased. The power pose is an expansive gesture (reminiscent of the expansive gestures of animals and human beings reflecting dominance and power) that takes up a lot of space and expands your body as you stretch out your arms and legs.

The psychology of the power pose is based on the concept that our behaviors drive our attitudes. Therefore, when you assume the power pose, an attitude of confidence and assertiveness is conveyed. Amy Cuddy, one of the proponents of the power pose, is a Harvard Business School professor. She says, *"Body-mind approaches such as power posing rely on the body, which has a more primitive and direct link to the mind, to tell you that you're confident."*

One of the most popular forms of power poses used to build confidence is the Wonder Woman pose. In this pose, you stand with your legs wide apart, hands on your hips, and the chin tilted slightly upward. This pose is very useful to adopt when you quickly want to build your level of assertiveness and confidence.

For example, suppose you have to give an important presentation to some senior managers in your office. You have prepared your presentation well. You have practiced really hard, and yet there is that inexplicable feeling of nervousness that is playing spoilsport.

During such times, the Wonder Woman power pose can do real wonders. Take a few minutes of solitude just before the presentation is due. Visit the restroom or find any other quiet spot. Close your eyes, focus on your breath, and physically balance yourself. Then, take the Wonder Woman power pose, and stand that way for a couple of minutes. Breathe gently, and feel the confidence rising in your body and mind. After you are satisfied with your efforts, relax, and go and make a success of your presentation.

Wrap-Up Tips to Build Assertiveness

The following points represent a short summary of the tips and tools you can use to build assertiveness (with input from this chapter and the previous one):

- You and your opinions are as valuable as everyone else's.
- Be sensible and fair in all your conversations and interactions.
- Be mindfully present in every interaction.
- Identify and practice the right (or normal) tone of voice in all uncomfortable situations.
- Don't be judgmental about anything or anyone because everyone is entitled to his or her opinion.
- Remember, your preferences, likes, and dislikes may be very different from those of other people. Being different does not mean inferior.
- Take valuable criticism seriously but not personally.

- Use the power of the Wonder Woman power pose to boost critical hormone levels that are connected to confidence and assertiveness.

Conclusion

This last chapter of the book is dedicated to listing some of the amazing benefits of assertiveness so that you can feel motivated to reread the book and redo the exercises in it to begin your journey of building assertiveness. Here are some benefits of building assertiveness:

You will not be taken for granted – Your ability to assertively state your views and opinions will ensure that no one will take you for granted; a common disadvantage with passive people.

Your popularity will soar – Your ability to listen to and accept others' viewpoints and opinions will attract more people to you, and your popularity will get a huge boost.

Your communication skills will improve considerably – Being assertive calls for developing your communication skills. As you learn and master new techniques, not only will your assertiveness get a boost, but your articulation skills will also see considerable improvement.

All your relationships will thrive – When you build your assertiveness, you also learn to respect and regard the thoughts and emotions of your partner, children, parents, colleagues, team members, and others. This positive attitude towards other people in your life will ensure that all your relationships thrive.

You will learn to manage your emotions maturely – Being assertive means you understand the havoc that unmanaged emotions can create in your life. This knowledge will drive you to learn how to manage your emotions well because of which you will handle any stressful situation with élan.

Now that you know the power of being assertive and its various benefits, it makes sense to reread the book and complete the exercises again so that you get a better understanding of how to plan your assertiveness-building path. So, go ahead, and dive head-on into the activity.

Also, you already know the deep connection that binds assertiveness to confidence and self-esteem. Therefore, if you want to receive more information and motivational tips and tricks to build confidence, self-esteem, and assertiveness, subscribe to our mailing list. Additionally, if you want to learn more about self-esteem and confidence, read the following books by the same author:

- [Self-Esteem for Women](#)
- [Confidence for Women](#)

Part 3: Self-Esteem for Women

Proven Techniques and Habits to Grow Your Self-Esteem, Assertiveness and Confidence in Just 60 Days

Chapter 1: Introduction - What is Self-Esteem?

Mary Angelou said, *"Success is liking yourself, liking what you do, and liking how you do it."* You have a high esteem of yourself when you attempt to achieve success in life on your terms.

Ask these questions of yourself:

- Are you proud of yourself?
- Do you like yourself the way you are?
- What are the topmost traits in you that make you proud?

If you are not able to answers these questions confidently or you feel uncomfortable having to answer them, then it is likely that you have low self-esteem. Before understanding why many of us have problems with self-esteem, we need to know the definition of self-esteem.

So, what is self-esteem? Self-esteem is a reflection of the respect and regard you have for yourself. A woman with a healthy level of self-esteem does not need external factors to feel good about herself. She does not need her husband telling her she looks good or that she is intelligent or that she's a good mother. She does not need her boss to tell her she does a great job at work.

Instead, a woman with a high level of self-esteem is keenly aware of her strengths and weaknesses. She accepts her strengths with pride, her weaknesses with humility, and is confident, assertive, and proud of her capabilities without being arrogant. She understands that she needs to work on her weaknesses and is happy to share the benefits of her strengths with others.

Self-esteem is an essential identity issue that is vital for joy and happiness in our lives. Self-esteem is needed to live and experience life joyfully. Once you achieve self-esteem, then it reflects in the way you handle life and its myriad challenges. Self-esteem can be defined in many ways including:

- A sense of self-worth and self-belief in one's own capabilities
- How good or bad you feel about yourself and your worth
- Your overall evaluation of your emotional, physical, and mental well-being

Signs of Low Self-Esteem

Look out for these signs that subtly or obviously reflect your low self-esteem:

You keep apologizing unnecessarily – This sign can be easily missed and misinterpreted for politeness. However, look again closely at instances when you have said sorry needlessly. For example, if you bump into someone accidentally, do you instinctively apologize without even seeing whose fault it was? If this is the case, you could be a victim of low self-esteem. Your apology could be rooted in a misconceived belief that everything that is going wrong is your fault.

You attribute everything to luck – If you get a promotion in your office, do you say, "I was lucky," or "I feel blessed?" If yes, this could mean that you don't know how to give credit to yourself for good results; a typical symptom of low self-esteem. You believe that something good happened to you not because you are worthy of it but because of divine intervention or luck. The belief in the divine is not an issue. Your lack of belief in your worth is a disturbing thought. You don't like to accept compliments and praise because of this lack of self-belief.

You do things that you don't really like – For example, you could be buying dresses that you are not really comfortable in or refurbishing your home in a way that is not your taste just to appear fashionable and trendy. Ask yourself how many times you have invited that girl whom you hate to all your parties. Ponder these choices and questions, and see if they are driven by a need to please others; this is another key element that reflects low self-esteem.

You are afraid of conflicts and making mistakes – If you hate having conflicts with anyone in your life, then it could be a sign of low self-esteem because you don't want to say anything that is confrontational. You hate to make mistakes because you are afraid of failures.

Other common signs of low self-esteem include sensitivity to criticism, social withdrawal, hostility (typically to hide the feeling of low self-esteem), and being excessively preoccupied with personal problems. Low self-esteem also is reflected through physical symptoms such as frequent headaches, fatigue, and insomnia.

Signs of High Self-Esteem

Here are some signs of high self-esteem:

- You are not afraid of making mistakes.
- You have no problems accepting compliments proudly but without arrogance.
- You are not overly sensitive to criticism.
- You are willing to take risks.
- You don't let others disrespect you or abuse you and your abilities.

Why Do Women have Low Self-Esteem?

The foundations for our self-esteem are laid at very early developmental stages. Much before our brains develop complex cognitive systems, we are exposed to feelings of shame, guilt, and pride through the interactions we have with our primary caregivers. These early-stage basic foundations influence the way we think of ourselves in our adulthood.

Additionally, girls seem to be at a disadvantage when it comes to self-esteem because our society 'expects' girls to behave 'nicely' whereas boys 'can be boys,' where misbehavior is seen as an unavoidable natural instinct. Therefore, girls experience failure and rejection with a lot more intensity than boys. Women think about their feelings of shame and guilt for a sustained period of time, enhancing their feelings of low self-esteem.

High expectations (such as those listed below) result in low self-esteem in women:

- Little girls are supposed to stay away from tussles and fights; those are reserved for the boys.

- Little girls are expected to avoid aggressive behaviors of all kinds to the extent that if they choose aggressive sports, then women are treated disdainfully.

- They are expected to behave nicely so that they are ready for matrimony; many times, this is at the cost of their dreams and desires.

- Women are expected to be 'perfect' in all ways. Many women reject those parts of themselves which are not aligned with societal expectations, meeting this bizarre and extremely unreasonable demand for perfection, resulting in low self-esteem.

- In the modern world, perfection includes having a 'perfect' body' too. Social media and print media are replete with movie stars, and their 'perfectly' toned bodies and unblemished faces drive the desire of the average women to reach those unreasonable levels. Marketers take advantage of these desires and sell unrealistic dreams to women. Self-esteem takes a big beating when women fail to achieve these dreams.

- And, if some women do manage to break these stereotypes and do well for themselves, they are expected to downplay their achievements and be modest, and not 'show off.'

- Women who talk proudly about their qualifications are called braggarts, whereas men talking about the same qualifications are called 'confident achievers.'

All these negativity-focused reasons drive uncertainty in women, and most of them are scared of or even unaware of their inherent abilities. Their self-talk focuses only on their weaknesses and inabilities, with little or no thought to their real powers and strengths. The final result is very low self-esteem.

Importance of Self-Esteem

High self-esteem uplifts you whereas low self-esteem drags you down. With high self-esteem, you will be able to achieve your highest potential and live life to please yourself. Of course, people with high self-esteem understand that pleasing oneself does not mean hurting others. It only means you are in the driver's seat of your life.

With high self-esteem comes high levels of confidence and assertiveness. Your belief in your capabilities and your acceptance of your weaknesses helps you to be confident and assert yourself without feeling arrogant or victimized.

Self-Discovery Questions on Your Current Level of Self-Esteem

Answer the following questions honestly, and you will get a fairly good idea of your current level of self-esteem. You can begin your journey to build your self-esteem from this place.

- Do you think you are a boring person?
- Do you think you are always messing up things?
- Do you believe your absence will be felt at a party or any social gathering?

- Do you think your loved ones don't trust your capabilities?
- Do you believe you are not worthy of anything?
- Do you take yourself to be a complete failure?
- Do you believe you can match the capabilities of other people in any given social setup?
- Do you think you can achieve your highest potential?
- Do you think you deserve to be loved?

Chapter 2: The Components of Building Self-Esteem

"Self-esteem is a powerful force within each of us … Self-esteem is the experience that we are appropriate to life and to the requirements of life," said Nathaniel Branden. He was a close associate of the highly celebrated author Ayn Rand and an eminent psychotherapist in his own right. Branden spoke at length about self-esteem and its six important components in his famous book, The Six Pillars of Self-Esteem.

The six pillars of self-esteem, according to Nathaniel Branden, include:

1. The Practice of Living Consciously
2. The Practice of Self-Acceptance
3. The Practice of Self-Responsibility
4. The Practice of Self-Assertiveness
5. The Practice of Living Purposefully
6. The Practice of Personal Integrity
7. Let's look at each of them in a little bit of detail.

The Practice of Living Consciously

How many times have you felt that you are drifting through life without knowing how you reached where you are now or where you are going next? You live each day like an automaton; eating, sleeping, doing the routine things and everything else without being conscious of your feelings and thoughts. This is the state of most women of the modern-day as they struggle to juggle their careers, homes, and many other social expectations.

Lao Tzu said, *"If you are depressed, you are living in the past. If you are anxious, you are living in the future. If you are at peace, you are living in the present."* Living consciously helps you live in the moment, helping you experience life more meaningfully than before.

A key element in living consciously is being acutely aware of your thoughts and emotions.

Take the example of cooking the evening meal for your family. Today, focus on your thoughts and emotions while your body is engaged in the cooking activity.

Are your thoughts about the cooking, the smells, the ingredients that are going into the dish, the measurement of these ingredients, the texture of the dish, etc.? Or are your thoughts on something that happened in the office during the day or an impending argument you are planning with your partner when he returns? Or are the thoughts simply random and you have no idea what you are thinking? Now, focus on the emotions while you are cooking. Are you happy? Sad? Angry? Just okay, with no particular feelings?

Cooking consciously requires you to focus your thoughts, emotions, and your entire being on that one activity. Your self-awareness increases when you indulge consciously in each of your tasks. When you are aware of every element that is occupying your body, mind, and spirit, you begin to see things that were hitherto invisible because you did not focus on them. With this newly widened perspective, you can manage difficult situations in a much better way than before.

Living consciously is the most important step to increase self-awareness, and with increased self-awareness comes self-improvement and improved self-esteem.

The Practice of Self-Acceptance

"Wanting to be someone else is a waste of the person you are," advised Marilyn Monroe, and acceptance of this one truth can positively impact the life of every woman on this planet. You are unique, beautiful, and complete in yourself. Chasing after things that take away this uniqueness is an unworthy and useless activity.

We saw how, when you live consciously, your level of self-awareness increases considerably. Being self-aware means you know your strengths, your capabilities, and your weaknesses. Self-acceptance simply means being fine with how you are right now.

So, you cook wonderfully, and your family loves every dish you turn out. Self-acceptance means accepting this trait proudly, but not with arrogance, which is not a difficult thing to do. Now, take, for example, a lack of great fashion sense. Accepting this weakness without a feeling of guilt and being okay with it is what self-acceptance is about.

Self-acceptance does not mean you will not work to overcome your weaknesses. In fact, self-acceptance does not mean liking or disliking a trait. It only means you are fine with how you are for the moment. Self-acceptance enhances self-love, and when you love yourself, you do not need anyone else to love you and make you complete. This sense of being complete is a significant contributor to your self-esteem.

Like Ayn Rand said, *"To say 'I love you,' one must be ready to say the 'I'!"* When you accept yourself the way you are, you will happily accept others the way they are, which will help you lead a far more harmonious life than before.

The Practice of Self-Responsibility

Self-responsibility is a sign of strength. Only powerful and strong people take responsibility for themselves and their lives. Mediocrity encourages blaming others, whereas excellence urges you to take control of your life.

Dr. Wayne Dyer, one of the influential thinkers of modern times, said, *"Everything you do is based on the choices you make. It's not your parents, your past relationships, your job, the economy, the weather, an argument, or your age that is to blame. You and only you are responsible for every decision and choice you make."*

You have learned to live consciously. You have learned the art of self-acceptance. The next step to improved self-esteem is to take responsibility for your life and sit in the driver's seat. Your happiness is in your hands. If you are sad, then you choose to be sad, as it is possible to find positivity even in the bleakest of situations.

Susan B. Anthony has a constitutional amendment named after her. She was one of the pioneers who fought for women's rights to vote in the US. She took responsibility for the wrongs happening in her life. She strongly believed in her right to vote and did not wait for men to come forward and fight for her. Although Susan B. Anthony did not live to see the beneficial outcome of her fight, her name is cast in stone in American history because the 19th Amendment, giving US women suffrage rights, is called the Susan B. Anthony Amendment.

It is important that you learn lessons from such powerful women and take responsibility for your life. For example, if you have a problem with your fashion sense, then take lessons from someone you trust. If there is no such person in your life, there are many grooming classes available where you can pick up this skill. The critical thing to self-responsibility is to stop blaming others for your problems, and instead, find ways to overcome them.

The Practice of Self-Assertiveness

Assertiveness is a critical personality trait that helps you win arguments and get some extra brownie points at a negotiation table. Assertiveness is an external trait that reflects the strength of your powers as well as the humility you have when it comes to accepting your weaknesses.

Self-assertiveness includes all the above plus a little more. Self-assertiveness calls for being true to yourself. It calls for reflecting your inner personality to the outside world. Self-assertiveness is the exact opposite of presenting a façade to the other people around you while you have a completely different personality within. It is the trait of authenticity. Self-assertiveness calls for living your dreams and desires the way you want to, and not to please someone else.

Dr. Elizabeth Blackwell was the first woman who graduated with a medical degree from an American medical college. If she had not the self-assertiveness qualities, the modern world, perhaps, would have to wait a little longer before women were allowed into medical schools to earn degrees and practice medicine.

"The most fundamental aggression to ourselves, the most

fundamental harm we can do to ourselves, is to remain ignorant by not having the courage and the respect to look at ourselves honestly and gently," says Pema Chodron, the celebrated American Tibetan Buddhist, and an ordained Buddhist nun.

Live consciously, accept yourself, take self-responsibility, and be self-assertive to build self-esteem slowly but steadily in a way that it will never leave your side. Self-assertiveness requires you to speak your mind even in the face of adversity and unpopularity.

For example, if you believe in disciplining your children from a young age, then there will be times when you will have to make unpopular calls that could make your children dislike or even hate you for a while. It is indeed a difficult thing for a mother to accept this situation. But, if your self-assertiveness is at a healthy level, then you will find the courage to handle this temporary unpleasantness and discipline. Your kids will thank you for it, later on. But, right now, you will need to be self-assertive to do what is best for your kids.

The Practice of Living with a Purpose

John F. Kennedy said, *"Efforts and courage are wasted without direction and purpose."* Look back at your life and think of the most glorious moments. Recall why the moments were so glorious that those feelings are deeply etched in your psyche. One of the prominent reasons that will stand out is that they were a moment of achieving a predetermined purpose.

Whether it was graduating college with flying colors, getting that coveted promotion, or helping your mother through a difficult illness, having a purpose enhances the joy of outcome. A purposeless life is like a rudderless ship that drifts along where the elements of nature choose to take it.

Your life undergoes a paradigm shift when you know the purpose that guides and drives you. The Triune Brain Model, proposed by Paul MacLean, the famed 1960s neuroscientist, says that the human brain consists of three parts including the reptilian or the instinctual part, the mammalian or the emotional part, and the primate or the thinking part.

The reptilian part of the brain handles things like territory and aggression. The mammalian part manages the food and sex. The primate or the thinking part handles deeper elements like complex concepts, perception, planning, etc. This primate part of the brain knows that you need meaning and purpose in your life for fulfillment.

Elizabeth Gilbert, the author of the international bestseller, *Eat, Pray, Love,'* discovered her purpose for writing while she was traveling to heal from a painful divorce. She traveled to Italy, India, and Bali in search of enjoyment, devotion, and balance. These travels helped her discover her purpose which, in turn, brought her success and happiness. Before that, she was living an average life, thinking she was happy in her marriage.

It is only when you put your mind to the concept of living purposefully that you can live life meaningfully and sublimely experience each moment. Life with a purpose will ensure you are not drifting along thoughtlessly merely going where circumstances choose to take you. You don't need to travel the world to find your life's purpose. Sit down with a pen and paper, and find answers to the self-assessment questions given at the end of this chapter to discover your real purpose in life.

A life purpose should be based on your dreams and desires, and not be passed on from influencers in your life like your parents, spouse, teachers, bosses, etc. Once you have clearly defined the primary purpose of your life, then you must endeavor to break it up into measurable, time-bound goals so that you can keep track of your progress and make suitable changes if needed.

The Practice of Personal Integrity

You can see how you have progressed in building your self-esteem. You started with learning to live consciously, then accepting yourself the way you are, warts and all; learned to take self-responsibility for your life and the choices you make; learned the importance of self-assertiveness; and then began living with a deep sense of purpose.

As you progress through each of the five pillars, you will find the strength of self-esteem building even as you enhance your self-awareness and become comfortable living life with yourself and on your terms. The sixth and the last pillar, namely "The Practice of Personal Integrity," gives an enormous amount of strength to your self-esteem.

Personal Integrity is living a life based on the values and principles you have chosen to be your guiding light. The more you lead a life that is aligned with those chosen personal values, the higher your self-esteem will grow. Living a life aligned with your values enhances your self-belief to lead a fulfilling and meaningful life, overcoming challenges on your own which, in turn, directly impacts self-esteem levels positively.

If Mother Teresa had not had the deep sense of personal

integrity needed to stand up for what she truly believed in, she could not have become the beacon of light for the most underprivileged people in India. Although a part of her life was dedicated to underprivileged Indians, her work in other parts of the world did not go unnoticed, which is why she has conferred the Nobel Peace Prize in 1979!

To practice personal integrity, you have to earn the 'unpopular' tag quite often. For example, if you have an office project to finish by the end of the day, you might have to say no to a get-together lunch with your colleagues because that will delay your work in the evening. Although these negative responses might be aligned with your personal integrity, they could make you unpopular with your colleagues, and it is possible that you might not get many invitations in the future.

The practice of personal integrity is a tough road to take as it can turn very lonely. However, this final pillar considerably enhances the power of your self-esteem.

Self-esteem is not about achieving perfection. It is the simple acceptance of yourself, including strengths and weaknesses. Self-esteem is accepting a particular situation and knowing that you are not equipped to handle it, and either choosing to seek help (if possible) or making choices that are aligned with your abilities. Self-esteem does not come from being confident in your current state of skills. It comes from your ability to learn and build new skills for self-improvement. To be in a constant state of learning, you have to move out of your comfort zone. The more you learn, the more confidence you will build which, in turn, will help in developing your self-esteem.

Self-Assessment Section

Answer the questions under each of the six components of

self-esteem. This exercise will help you gauge your current status on all of them. You can use the self-knowledge gained from these self-assessment exercises to create an effective and efficient plan to develop your self-esteem.

Self-Questions to Gauge Your Present State of Conscious Life

1. Did you choose your career consciously, or did you take it simply because it came your way?
2. Do you do jobs that are given to you, or do you pick up jobs that you love to do?
3. Are you doing activities simply to fill up your waking hours, or are you doing activities that give you joy and happiness?
4. Are you conscious of the progress of time, or do you just drift through the day, uncertain of how you spend your waking hours?
5. Do you focus on each activity to identify and appreciate how it is contributing to your growth, or do you unconsciously do each task thoughtlessly?
6. Are you aware of how your money is being spent, or do you simply live from one paycheck to the next?

Self-Questions to Gauge Your Present State of Self-Acceptance

1. Are you living life to meet your desires or someone else's?
2. Do you forgive yourself easily?
3. Do you love yourself enough to know you should begin

to look after yourself?

4. Do you accept yourself enough to know that you need good food, exercise, and sufficient rest to lead a fulfilling life?

5. Do you accept your past mistakes by letting them go out of your life?

6. Do you accept yourself so that you can commit to things you know you can achieve and say no to things you know you cannot achieve?

7. Do you give yourself sufficient me-time during which you indulge in activities with yourself?

8. Are you comfortable when you are alone?

Self-Questions to Gauge Your Present State of Self-Responsibility

1. Do you believe you give your best in everything you do? If no, write down the reasons.

2. Do you believe you set reasonably high standards for yourself so that you can improve yourself? If no, why not?

3. Do you start any work with the feeling, "Oh! This is impossible to do?" If yes, ask yourself why?

4. Do you believe you take sufficient time and effort to do all your tasks in the best possible way? If no, why not?

5. Do you believe you are doing enough to prevent distractions, procrastination, and temptations from getting the better of you? If no, why not?

6. Do you believe you optimally use all the resources available to you? If no, what is stopping you?

7. Do you believe you seek help when you need it? If no, why not?

8. Do you believe you review your work to ensure errors are minimized? If no, why not?

9. Do you believe you do research and find the best solutions for the various problems in your life? If no, why not?

Self-Questions to Gauge Your Present State of Self-Assertiveness

1. Do you think you say yes often, even when you want to say no?

2. Do you think you hide your thoughts and emotions if the person you are speaking to is a stranger?

3. Are you afraid to give negative feedback because you don't like to be unpopular?

4. Do you believe it is easier to pretend to say something nice even if it is not true?

5. Do you think that in your efforts to keep everyone happy, you are contradicting yourself?

6. Do you think you are comfortable in face-to-face interaction?

Self-Questions to Gauge Your Present State of Living Purposefully

1. Do you think your purpose in life is your own or

borrowed from your parents?

2. Can you clearly talk about the journey of your life until now, and where you are headed in the future?

3. Is your perception about yourself based on others' perceptions about yourself? For example, do you believe you are a 'bad' cook because your mother thought so? Or that you are 'bad' at math because your teacher in your school thought so?

4. Do you think you are walking a life path that you truly believe in?

5. Do you know your life's purpose?

6. Where do you see yourself five or ten years from now? Have you written down your goals?

7. Do you keep track of the progress you have made?

Self-Questions to Gauge Your Present State of Personal Integrity

1. Do you believe that, in today's society, we have to cheat or lie to succeed?

2. Do you think that people who take ethical shortcuts succeed more than those who choose not to?

3. Are you happy with your level of ethics and personal integrity?

4. Do you think you can lie about your home address if it is the only way to get your child admitted to a good school?

5. Do you think you are doing enough to build personal

integrity in your children?

6. Do you often lie to your friends and family?

7. Do you often lie to your bosses and colleagues?

8. Do you show exaggerated expense claims for any overseas office trips?

Chapter 3: Habits and How to Use Them for the Good

Charles Duhigg is a bestselling author and Pulitzer Prize winner, and one of his most famous work is titled, *The Power of Habit."* In this book, Charles Duhigg talks at length about the habit loop and how it is possible to fit any habit into this loop which includes three elements, namely:

1. The Cue
2. The Routine
3. The Reward

This chapter is dedicated to giving you some insights into these three elements of the habit loop, and how you can use them to get rid of old bad habits and replace them with new good ones. Let's look at each of these three elements of the habit loop.

The Cue

The cue is the trigger that puts your brain into automatic mode and brings in the specific routine. The cue initiates the habitual behavior or routine. The trigger for setting in the habit can be a person, a location, emotion, or anything else. It is challenging to identify the cue(s) that trigger the routine of any particular habit. Changing a bad habit requires you to first identify the cue(s).

Fortunately, psychologists have categorized all cues into five basic types including time, location, a preceding event, emotional state, and other people. Let us look at each of the five types in a bit of detail to help you identify what is triggering your bad habit.

The time cue – This is the most common cue for any habit. Look at your daily schedule, and you will understand why time is the most common cue for habits. You wake up at a particular time, have your meals at specific times, go to bed at a certain time, etc. Now let us look at an example of a bad habit that depends on the time cue.

Suppose you go for your morning coffee break at 11 a.m. each day. You join your colleagues in the office cafeteria. Your coffee always includes a doughnut or a cookie, which is causing weight gain. You want to stop this habit of eating a cookie or doughnut during this break. When you recognize the cue, you can make changes so that you respond differently to that cue.

So, your cue is the 11 a.m. break. Instead of going to the cafeteria, you can choose to drink your coffee at your desk so that you are not tempted to have the doughnut or cookie. Or, you can carry a box of freshly-cut fruits which you can have during the break.

The location cue – This is another powerful habit creator. You automatically turn on the light when you enter a particular room. You automatically shut the bathroom door once you are inside. All these actions or routines are habitual, and your brain kicks the routine in as soon as it recognizes the location cue.

How many times have you walked into your kitchen to unwittingly reach out for the cookie jar or chips container? That is the power of the location cue. It is so deeply ingrained in your psyche that your brain automatically drives your sense organs to perform the routine; in this case, reaching out for the cookie jar.

Here is a classic way of using the power of the habit to do something healthy. Instead of cookies, place some fruit in the jar. So, when you reach your hand into the jar, you get healthy fruit instead of cookies. Alternately, put the cookie jar somewhere that is not easily accessible.

Therefore, identifying the cue has given you solutions that facilitate the change of habit or eliminating the habit.

The preceding event cue – When your phone rings, don't you automatically pick it up? After you finish your call, don't you invariably look for an email or social media notifications? That is a classic example of a preceding event cue.

You can use this cue to build great habits. For example, you can choose to wait for your phone to ring at least four times before picking it up. Focus on your breath while you wait to pick up your phone. This approach will prepare you for managing the call more effectively, irrespective of who the call is from. Every time your phone rings create a habit of focusing on your breath.

You may not be able to concentrate on more than one or two inhalations and exhalations. However, even this small habit can be of immense help because your brain is now being attuned to something positive. In fact, this approach slows you down, which is a good thing in this modern, rushing, hither-thither world.

Another great example of a preceding event cue: While you wait for your morning coffee to brew, invariably you are checking your phone again or letting your thoughts go randomly all over the place. Use these couple of minutes to meditate. Focus on your thoughts and emotions and be mindful of them. This morning meditation sets the perfect tone for the entire day.

One more example that all of us can easily relate to is eating while watching TV. Before you switched on the TV, you were not hungry and did not want to eat anything. As soon as you sit on the couch and turn on the power button on the TV remote, your brain goes into eating mode. Without even pausing to think, you have walked into the kitchen and brought out a bag of chips to munch on while watching TV.

Identify and recognize this common precedent event cue, and find ways not to indulge in eating while watching TV. One option is not to watch TV until your brain is rewired not to relate to the TV watching with binge-eating. Another option is to ensure you have no junk food lying around at home. Instead, stock your fridge with fruits and vegetables to make yourself a healthy salad to munch on while you watch TV.

The emotional state cue – Your emotional state is more often a trigger for a bad habit than a good one. For example, when you are depressed, do you binge-eat? When you are angry, do you scream and shout? When you are upset, do you shop for unnecessary things? All these are classic examples of emotional state cues.

The problematic thing about emotion-based cues is that they are very tough to control because, during a heightened emotional state, your feelings are bound to overwhelm and rule you. It takes a lot of effort to manage emotions to prevent them from overwhelming you.

Therefore, in the initial stages of identifying bad habits based on this kind of cue, it is best to avoid trying to replace them with a good habit. An excellent way to manage these conditions is to practice mindfulness. As your feelings engulf you, step outside of them, and watch the emotions as objectively as you can. Let yourself think, "Yes, I am angry because ..." However, try and not respond to their feelings. Just watch them as a witness.

Initially, this method is going to be tough because you are habituated to reacting to your emotions. However, with patient and persistent practice, you will see that this method of observing your emotions without reacting to them becomes increasingly easy.

Soon, you will notice that emotions are one of the most transient aspects of human nature. A situation that triggered anger in you yesterday may make you laugh out loud today. Mindfulness helps you recognize these emotional states, and when you focus on the feelings, the brain is prevented from going into automatic mode.

The 'other people' cue – Jim Rohn, a highly influential American author, entrepreneur, and motivational speaker, says, *"You are the average of the five people you spend the most time with."* It is very easy to verify this observation in your life.

Have you noticed how much you eat when you have your meal with people who overeat? If you had been mindful, would you have seen that you eat far more than your usual amount? Similarly, if you are having a meal with people who eat consciously, you will also unwittingly follow their habits. This is how 'other people' affect the way you form your habits.

For example, if you don't usually drink, but are in the company of friends who drink, it is natural to get yourself a drink. This attitude is only a response to the environment and the behavior of the people around you. If you can identify such 'other people' in your life who influence bad habits, it makes sense to stay away from them as much as possible.

The Routine

The routine is the actual habit, which could be emotional, physical, or mental. The routine part of the loop is easily recognizable. For example, eating that cookie during your morning break or when you visit the kitchen is the routine.

The Reward

The reward is the end result that appears worthwhile for your brain to set up the habit formation or the remembering and recalling routine for future use. The 'reward' is a misnomer in a bad habit. In truth, there is no reward because bad habits result in emotional, financial, and physical losses. However, the brain (driven by the 'sense of temporary satisfaction' given by the habit) believes the 'reward' is worthwhile and creates the habit loop so that the automatic mode is set in once the cue comes into play.

Therefore, to break bad habits, you must try and experiment with different rewards that are truly worthwhile so that your brain creates the loop for good habits. For example, runners get a 'high' while running and gamblers get the same 'high' while gambling. So, if you can replace running with gambling, your brain will believe it is worthwhile to run and will create the remembering and recalling loop for the good habit.

The Importance of Identifying the Habit Loop

Identifying the habit loop in each of your habits can help you manage your habits more positively than before in two ways:

- Cues can help in creating new good habits
- Cues can help in breaking and/or replacing bad habits

Changing habits is tough. However, identifying the habit loop simplifies the process of giving up bad habits and creating new ones. Identifying the structure of a habit helps you find solutions to make positive changes in your life. Essentially, identifying your habit loops enhances your self-awareness which, in turn, enables you to find innovative solutions to overcome bad habits.

Replacing Old Bad Habits with New Good Ones

"Depending on what they are, our habits will either make us or break us. We become what we repeatedly do." —Sean Covey. Therefore, it makes sense to eliminate bad habits and create good habits.

Eliminating old bad habits is really not possible because the worth of the reward associated with the habit is deeply etched in our brains. For example, flopping on the couch after returning from work can never really be eradicated from your mind because neurological patterns are already in place.

However, if you can construct new neurological patterns that deliver the same level of satisfaction as flopping on the couch, then these old patterns will get replaced with the new ones. For example, if you quickly begin your walk or run after returning from work, then your brain will slowly but surely replace this neurological pattern over the old one, helping you overcome the bad habit and create a new good one.

The trick is to keep the same cue and reward (because these two cannot really be changed) and experiment with new and worthier routines than the earlier ones to replace bad habits with good ones. So, in the above example, the cue is a combination of time and location—the location is the couch after returning from work, and the reward is the satisfaction received from the happy chemicals. The routine is flopping on the couch.

Now, keep the cue and reward constant, and instead of flopping on the couch, go for a run or visit the gym. Effectively, you have broken the bad habit and replaced it with a good habit.

Self-Assessment Questions On Your Current Level of Habits

Answer the following questions which will help you understand your current level of habits:

1. Do you believe you are a dependable worker?
2. Do you think you are a dependable mother, relentlessly doing all the regular activities needed for your children?
3. Do you believe you are a punctual person?
4. Are you a great collaborator, ensuring team meetings are held productively?

5. Do you think you are a disciplined and responsible worker who does not need to be supervised?

6. Can you recognize the top five bad habits you are keen on getting rid of?

Chapter 4: Practical Examples

We discussed the six components of self-esteem in Chapter 2 and how it is important to build each one of them to take your self-esteem up a few notches. This chapter is dedicated to giving you some tips, based on practical examples, to develop the six components.

The Practice of Living Consciously

NLP Techniques

Neuro-Linguistic Programming or NLP is designed to align your subconscious and unconscious minds with your conscious mind so that your entire being is moving harmoniously in the same direction. NLP stands for:

- Neuro – relates to the brain's nerves and the neuro-systems

- Linguistic – relates to the language of the mind

- Programming – makes something work in a particular way

Here are a couple of popular NLP techniques to help you live more consciously than before.

Focus on your thoughts – Our subconscious and unconscious minds are deeply affected by our thoughts. For example, if you think that you are not going to get that promotion, then your conscious mind and your physical body will resist your attempts to prepare for the promotion because your negative thoughts are forcing your deeper mind to believe the thought to be true.

However, if your thoughts are, "I deserve that promotion, and I will definitely get it," then your subconscious mind will believe this to be true and will drive your conscious mind and your physical body to work hard and achieve your promotion.

Prayers – Prayers represent your wishes and hopes. Prayers render a deep sense of faith that there is a higher power that is working with you to help you realize your dreams.

For example, if you pray for your son to do well on his SAT exams, then your subconscious mind feels empowered to encourage your son to work hard and believe in his capabilities to achieve success. Your faith in your son's capabilities and strengths will pass on to him, urging him to give his best, considerably enhancing his chances for success.

Affirmations

Affirmations empower you to believe in yourself and your abilities to achieve success. Use the following positive affirmations to live more consciously than before:

- I am my own master and need no one else to be complete
- I use my energies constructively and productively
- I feel happy when I make conscious choices and live life on my terms
- I am acutely tuned in to my thoughts and emotions.

Visualization

Davin Alexander is a famous author of many bestselling cookbooks and a TV reality show hostess. She is a firm believer in creating vision boards to help her achieve her dreams. She says creating your dreams into a visual in your mind is a powerful reminder of your future dreams and goals.

Visualization is nothing but a vision board in your mind. All of us have a powerful imagination and it makes sense to use it effectively to live consciously. Visualize victories and happy days. Work towards crystallizing those mind visuals.

Meditation

Meditation is about spending time with your thoughts and emotions. When you meditate, you are focusing on your feelings and thoughts, many times even unpleasant ones too. When you connect with these emotions and thoughts, you get to know them better and discern between the useful and wasteful ones so you can discard the bad ones and put good thoughts to effective use.

Start and end your day with a ten-minute meditation. During this meditation, visualize how your day will unfold, and prepare yourself for the expected good and bad events. You can also use positive affirmations during your meditation session.

Maintaining a Diary

Maintaining a diary facilitates improved conscious living in multiple ways:

First, it enhances the experiences of the day as you relive them while making entries in your diary. For example, if your boss paid you a compliment, it is possible that you were so busy that you did not have time to revel in the joy. When you make this entry in your diary at the end of the day, you can recall this event and experience the happiness of the moment in a more wholesome manner than earlier.

You can feel the happiness for having worked hard and gotten praise from your boss. Now, if you remember that someone else in your team should also get a piece of this goodwill, then this might be the best time to pass on the compliments to that person too. It is natural to have forgotten to mention this team member's name to your boss when he said those nice things earlier in the day.

Second, maintaining a diary enhances your sense of gratitude as well. Being grateful for small things helps you live more consciously than before.

And finally, you can look at the negative experiences of the day with detachment, learn from them, and move on.

The Practice of Self-Acceptance

NLP Techniques

Anchoring for self-acceptance – Whenever you feel overwhelmed by some weakness, you need to reassure yourself that your strengths are sufficiently good to make up for this weakness. Anchoring is an amazing NLP technique that helps you recall happy moments by connecting them to a physical gesture.

For example, recall a happy memory, and as you relive the experience, rub the tips of your thumb and forefinger together. Every time you think of this memory, perform this gesture so that the experience is 'anchored' in your brain. Whenever you doubt yourself, repeat this action, and the positive image will fill your head, and you will regain control of your positivity.

Affirmations

Self-acceptance is an important element of self-esteem. Use any of the following affirmations for self-acceptance:

- I am worthy of happiness, joy, and love
- I will be loved only when I love myself
- I am unique, and that is the best thing about me
- I love myself unconditionally, and therefore, I can love others the same way
- I completely approve of myself
- I do not need anything or anyone other than myself to make me complete
- I will use the gift of life with confidence and exuberance
- I will surround myself with positivity because I deserve only that

Visualization

Always visualize yourself in a smiling and happy mood. Always focus on the good things in your life and visualize them. Automatically, you will get a smile on your face, and a smiling face will never fail to attract positivity and happy people and situations.

For example, when you think of something nice and pleasant, a smile comes up on your face without even you realizing it. Similarly, when you think of a terrible incident in your life, then either your face gets a frown or tears well up. Similarly, when you love and accept yourself the way you are, your confidence will reflect in your body language, taking your self-esteem a few notches up.

Meditation

Use the self-acceptance affirmations given above and meditate on them regularly so that your conscious, subconscious, and unconscious minds are all aligned with each other, helping you live a more harmonious and happy life than before.

Maintaining a Diary

Use the following prompts to make entries in your diary:

- What are the things that I have in my life that I know I deserve completely?
- How can I trust myself more?
- Was there an incident in your life that you believed was not right when it took place? However, now you know it was for the best. Write down the details of that incident.

The Practice of Self-Responsibility

NLP Techniques

The Swish technique – The Swish technique is used to convert negative thoughts into positive ones. Let us take a typical scenario in your life to explain it. Suppose you are having a dinner party. You are an excellent cook, and yet, your mind is full of doubts about whether all the dishes will turn out well. The Swish technique has three components, including:

The unwanted thought or trigger – This is the negative, self-doubting thoughts about your cooking skills.

The unwanted feeling – This is the feeling of fear and insecurity that comes with the negative trigger.

The replacement thought – Now, think of a time when you received great praise for your cooking skills. Replace the negative trigger with happy thoughts associated with the earlier success. Keep replacing the unwanted triggers with replacement thoughts until your mind is rewired to think positively.

The Swish NLP technique works excellently to eliminate baseless doubts in your mind so that you can take responsibility for yourself to work hard and achieve great outcomes.

Affirmations

Here are some powerful affirmations for personal responsibility:

- I take full responsibility for all the choices and experiences in my life.
- Only I am responsible for my life.
- I am not responsible for others' perceptions of me.
- I am entirely accountable for my actions, feelings, words, and thoughts, irrespective of what triggered them.

Visualization

Visualization of a future event or of a future time in your life helps you build self-responsibility to work towards achieving it. Here is an example of how to use visualization:

- First, find a calm place and sit comfortably.

- Next, close your eyes, and imagine how you see yourself five years from today.

- What do you see? A promotion? A happy home, filled with the joyous laughter of your loving children? Traveling the world? Pick one that is the most important for you.

- At this stage, don't doubt that you will achieve what you see in your mind. Simply fill in all the details in the image, and feel the visual coming to life. Etch this image in your mind.

- Open your eyes, and feel the joy of the visualization experience.

- Take responsibility for this dream, and begin your work to achieve it.

Meditation

Whenever something goes wrong in your life, your mind gets filled with negative thoughts, and by default, you choose to find someone else to blame. Don't be ashamed of this reaction. This is natural. However, when you live consciously, you will be acutely aware of this feeling.

Now, sit down comfortably, and relive the negative experience with your eyes closed. Remember to keep out the emotions during the meditation. Let us take an example. Suppose you were asked to do a presentation by your boss, and you did what you believed was right.

Now, the presentation does not go as well as it should have. Your boss gets angry and says something nasty to you in front of your colleagues. You could blame your boss for not checking your work earlier. However, that is not a healthy sign of taking self-responsibility.

Instead of reacting with anger, ask for permission and leave the meeting for a few minutes. Go to a calm place and reflect on the experience. Ask yourself the following questions:

- Why did you not ask for clarification and confirm whether your line of thought aligned with your boss' expectations?
- Why did you not ask your boss to look at your work and request feedback so that you could have made the corrections ahead of time?

Focus on the entire experience, and take self-responsibility for those elements that you could have done right, without waiting for anyone else. This approach will let you take control of your life and do the right things in the future. Mistakes are not to be taken personally, even if they come with some humiliation. Take mistakes in the right spirit, learn from them, and let them go.

Maintaining a Diary

At the end of each day, write two things that went wrong during the day. Recall the experiences and relive them in your mind, minus the emotions. Now, beside each of these experiences, write at least two ways you could have done something different so that the outcomes would not have been as bad as they turned out. Repeat this exercise every day, and you will notice how the power of self-responsibility improves the quality of your life.

The Practice of Self-Assertiveness

NLP Techniques

Learning to say no is one of the most critical lessons taught in NLP. Self-assertiveness calls for you to say no quite often in your life. How many times have you babysat for your neighbor while she partied with her friends simply because you couldn't find the courage to say no? How many times have you accepted more work than you can manage because you do not know how to say no or are scared you will lose your favorite spot in your boss' mind?

All these are classic examples of failing to practice self-assertiveness. You know saying no is the right thing to do, and it is aligned with your values and principles. And yet, fearing the unpopularity tag, you choose to be bullied into taking on more than your capability. Instead of losing out on self-assertiveness, build the necessary skills to become more assertive.

One of the most popular NLP techniques to learn how to say no is deconstructing and formulating desired scenarios. Practice responses and reactions in your mind, and use them in real-life scenarios. For example, if you have to say no to your neighbor the next time she asks for you to babysit her child while she goes partying, think of appropriate responses as to how you will deal with her in your mind. Formulate compelling answers to her expected counter-questions and practice them in your mind. The more you practice, the easier it will be to use them in real-life scenarios.

Affirmations

Repeat these affirmations to develop a natural sense of self-assertiveness so that you can express your emotions and thoughts honestly. These affirmations help in building your mental strength to increase your self-assertiveness.

- I am not afraid to speak my mind.
- I am an assertive person.
- I readily let others know my feelings.
- I am very confident when speaking to others.
- I stand firm and resolute when my core values are challenged.
- I stand up for my principles.
- I am confident in controlling my responses and reactions in any situation.
- I express myself honestly and strongly.
- I set clear standards and boundaries.
- I am respected for my self-assertiveness.

Visualization

Let us take an example of a situation wherein you have to give a presentation to your senior bosses. You are a great worker and that is why you have been chosen for this task. And yet, your lack of self-assertiveness skills puts you into a panic mode. Here is where visualization techniques will be of immense help.

First, make sure you are thoroughly prepared with your presentation. Practice repeatedly so that the presentation is deeply ingrained in your mind and you know it by rote, without any mistakes. Next, sit comfortably and close your eyes.

Visualize the room where all your seniors are sitting, waiting for you to start the presentation. Imagine yourself taking a deep breath and diving right into the presentation. In your mind, repeat the entire speech as if you are really giving it. Practice answers for expected counter-arguments from your seniors. Visualize confidence in your stance and gestures. Don't forget to visualize the smile on your face.

When you have finished giving the presentation, imagine your seniors congratulating you on a job well done. Now, open your eyes, and let the feeling of confidence in your visualization course through your body. Repeat this visualization until your brain is rewired for self-assertiveness.

Meditation

When you meditate, you are connected with your thoughts and emotions very deeply. This deep connection helps you discern between productive and unproductive thoughts. You can clearly see what went wrong in a particular situation, empowering you to handle them better in the future.

Meditation also helps you know the difference between aggression and assertiveness. You can fine-tune and alter your responses suitably when you realize this difference, thereby enhancing your level of self-awareness. With meditation comes calmness and peace which, in turn, empowers you to respond instead of reacting to difficult situations. You can use affirmations as mantras during your meditation sessions.

Maintaining a Diary

Make the following entries in your diary each day:

- The problems you experienced during the day.

- A suitable affirmation for each of the problems.

- Details of a mind-image for a better outcome than what you had.

For example, suppose your worst problem on a particular day was to get your project report all wrong. It was a mistake on your part, of course. However, your boss's reaction was quite rude and humiliating. You made the necessary corrections on the report, and the day finally ended.

Now, when you get home, write down three suitable affirmations for today's bad experience:

- My performance cannot be undermined by one correctable mistake.

- My boss' nasty reaction is a reflection of his nastiness and has nothing to do with me.

- Feeling bad and humiliated is a natural reaction, and I don't feel guilty or ashamed of it.

Next, visualize the same scene but imagine yourself standing up for your rights. For example, you could say, "Boss, I am sorry I made this mistake. However, it is a small and correctable one and does not really affect the overall picture. I don't believe it calls for a reaction that results in humiliation for me." While it might not make sense to speak like this in front of your colleagues, do visualize speaking to him in private, and letting him know that you were hurt by needless insults.

The Practice of Living with Purpose

NLP Techniques

A powerful NLP tool for living life purposefully is to set and follow SMART goals. SMART stands for:

S – Specific; for example, "By the end of this quarter, I will work hard and lose five pounds," is a specific and clear goal, unlike something as vague as "I will lose weight."

M – Measurable; In the above example, five pounds is measurable, whereas the second unspecific goal is not measurable; goals that do not have measurable aspects are not SMART goals.

A – Achievable; for example, "By the end of this quarter, I will work hard and lose five pounds," is an achievable goal, especially if you have a good weight-loss program ready to be followed and implemented. However, "I will take over my boss' role by this quarter," is not achievable because it requires other uncontrollable factors to play a part.

R – Realistic; for example, losing five pounds in three months is highly realistic if you stick to your plans. However, setting a goal of losing thirty pounds in three months is highly unrealistic, and cannot be given the label of being a SMART goal. Instead, you must break down the thirty pounds into five-pound installments.

T – Time-bound; your goals must have an expiry date. For example, losing five pounds in three months is time-bound, whereas "I will lose weight" has no time limit, and therefore cannot be a SMART goal.

Affirmations

Use the following affirmations to live life purposefully:

- My entire being is infused with a deep sense of purpose.
- All my actions and choices are aligned with my purpose.
- As I connect deeply with my soul, my life's purpose becomes increasingly clear.
- I find my body and mind filled with joy and happiness as I live my life with purpose.
- Each day, my purpose gets clearer than before.
- Every choice I make and every action I take brings me closer to my purpose.

Visualization

Choose your life purpose first, and then use any of the visualization techniques to help you achieve your dreams and desires:

- Imagine the day when your coveted promotion is announced. Visualize yourself being greeted and congratulated by your colleagues, team members, and your boss. Feel the pride of receiving the much-awaited reward.
- Visualize yourself participating in a high-level corporate seminar, and making a big success of your presentation.
- Imagine looking at your bank statement with a big credit that is your bonus for the year. Don't hesitate to

put a figure in your mind, and imagine the amount being credited to your account.

- Imagine yourself traveling the world and seeing beautiful places and writing about it in your blog.

- Visualize a happy home with the smells of cooking, the barking of a dog, the laughter of children, and other such beautiful things filling your home.

Powerful visualizations are great tools that effectively enhance your resolve and willpower to work hard and achieve your life's purpose.

Meditation

You need to continuously remind yourself of your life's purpose. Otherwise, it is bound to get lost in the din and noise of your daily routine. Your days are filled with work and activities that you hardly get time to spend with yourself, and in such a scenario, it is very easy to forget your life's purpose. In fact, if you don't keep track of your progress, you will see that your choices are counter-productive to your purpose.

Meditation is one of the best ways to keep reminding yourself of your life goals. As soon as you wake up, or before retiring to bed, sit for a few minutes in complete silence and solitude and repeat your life goal to yourself as a mantra or affirmation. For example, when the alarm wakes you up in the morning, don't jump out of bed immediately. Turn off the alarm, lie back on your bed, close your eyes, and repeat your life's purpose a couple of times. It could be anything, including:

- I promise to achieve my coveted promotion this year.

- I promise to work hard to earn more money to get myself that beautiful diamond ring.

- My life's purpose is to buy a beautiful home for my family.

Maintaining a Diary

You have already got your SMART goals in place by now. They are best recorded in your diary with sufficient space to make recordings of failed and successful milestones. Maintaining a diary is a great way to keep track of your progress and to know how much further you have to go before you achieve your life's purpose.

Maintaining a diary also keeps you alert and grounded. For example, suppose you have recently failed to achieve a particular milestone and are compelled to redo the effort. It is natural to feel discouraged and depressed during such difficult phases. Pick up your diary and read some of your success stories to feel motivated and rejuvenated.

Similarly, sometimes a string of successes can go to your head, and it is easy to let arrogance take control of your life. During such times, take a peek into your diary again, and reread the failures as a reminder to yourself that failure can come at any time during your life. Maintaining a diary, therefore, helps you to be grateful for your successes and the lessons learned from your failures.

The Practice of Personal Integrity

NLP Techniques

Personal integrity requires you to be true to your inner self. You practice what you preach and believe in. Leading a life of personal integrity requires a deep level of self-awareness regarding your values and principles. Some NLP tips to practice personal integrity:

- Don't be afraid to say no. Only then can you make those promises you can keep.

- Enhance your self-discipline so that you spend more time being productive rather than wasting time on valueless activities.

- Break down big goals into small, measurable, and timebound tasks for easy monitoring and ensuring that the final goal is reached in a systematic and disciplined way.

Affirmations

The following affirmations will help align your heart, mind, and body with your core values, thereby allowing you to practice personal integrity throughout your life:

- Everything I say or do is a sincere promise.

- I value integrity and honesty above all else.

- I practice what I preach.

- I do not have a problem accepting my mistakes and learning from them.

- I always do the right thing, even in the face of unpopularity and dissension.

- I make only those promises that I can keep.

Visualization

Perform visualization techniques that reflect scenes in which you keep your promises and imagine the smiles on the faces of the positively-affected individuals. For example, suppose you promise to take your kids out for a weekend picnic and your boss then calls you into work. The choices you make in such situations reflect your level of personal integrity. Always think and make your choices.

Meditation

Meditation increases our self-awareness. Self-awareness helps us understand and appreciate our core values which, in turn, helps us practice personal integrity with greater intensity than before. Meditation allows you to get connected with the deepest parts of your mind and the reasons behind your current personality and state of life and why you believe in your chosen core values. This knowledge makes it easy for you to practice personal integrity.

Meditation also keeps your mind clear of useless, confusing, and unproductive thoughts. A calm and clear mind offers a strong foundation to practice personal integrity.

Maintaining a Diary

Maintaining a diary helps you keep track of the times when you end up breaking promises despite your best efforts. Whenever you have had to break a promise, either knowingly or unwittingly, make a note in your diary and keep reading these journal entries. Don't forget to include the description of the sad or upset faces of the affected people when you broke the promise, and your feeling of disappointment in yourself.

When a similar situation comes up in your life where you are on the brink of breaking a promise, go back and reread these instances. The description of the sadness and your disappointment will ensure you try and avoid a similar situation and will motivate you to keep your promise.

Chapter 5: Workbook

This workbook is aligned with the format of the six components explained with practical examples in Chapter 4. Completing the workbook requires a bit of time and effort. However, it will be worthwhile for you as the exercise will help you increase your self-awareness which, in turn, will help you increase your self-esteem slowly but surely. This workbook has a general outlook and can be used by anyone.

Before you attempt the workbook, you must complete the self-assessment quizzes and questions given in Chapter 2, which describes the six components of self-esteem in a bit of detail. Arrange the six components in increasing order of importance in your life. For example, if you believe that your current status in the practice of living purposefully is at the lowest level, start this workbook from that element.

Workbook for the Practice of Living Consciously

NLP Techniques – Focus on Your Thoughts

Before going to bed, make a note of the three most critical thoughts that occupied your mind today:

1) _____
___

2) _____
___

3)
_____

—

NLP Techniques – Prayers

At the end of every week, make a note of the three most crucial wishes that you want to come true in the coming week:

1)
_____

—

2)
_____

—

3)
_____

—

Affirmations – Make a note of the three most vital affirmations aligned with your efforts to live consciously:

1) _____

2) _____

3) _____

Visualization – Visualize the one most important goal that you want to achieve within a year, and make detailed notes, including:

The scene

_____

The people in it

Smells
_____

Sounds
_____

Your feelings
_____

Meditation – When you complete your meditation session, what are the two most compelling thoughts that disturbed your meditation? Make a note of these two thoughts.

1)
_____

2)
_____

Maintaining a diary –Make a habit of reading your diary every week. Then, identify one element that was repeated at least twice for which you showed gratitude. If there was more than one, write all of them down:

1)
_____

–

Workbook for the Practice of Self-Acceptance

NLP anchoring technique - Take two of the most beautiful memories in your life. Create anchoring techniques for these experiences and practice them so that you can quickly retrieve them when needed.

1)
_____

2)
_____

Affirmations – Think for yourself and make a note of three affirmations for self-acceptance:

1)
_____

2)_____

3)_____

Visualization – Can you imagine yourself happy? Write a detailed scene of one such happy moment in your life.

_____

Meditation – Meditate on any of the affirmations for self-acceptance that you created for yourself. Alternately, you can use one of the following:

- I love myself unconditionally
- I accept my weaknesses with humility and my strengths with joy

Workbook for the Practice of Self-Responsibility

The NLP Swish technique – What are the three most painful unwanted triggers? Identify replacement triggers for each of them:

Unwanted trigger 1)

Replacement trigger 1)

_____

Unwanted trigger 2)

_____

Replacement trigger 2)

_____

Unwanted trigger 3)

_____

Replacement trigger 3)

_____

Affirmation – Write three self-responsibility affirmations of your own.

1) _____

2) _____

3) _____

Visualization – Think of the most important goal of your life. Now, imagine the day you will achieve it. Make detailed notes of this visualization.

_____

Meditation – Recall a painful event in your life. Relive the experience, minus the attached emotions, and write down the various reasons for it. Make two categories of the contributing factors:

Under your control

_____

Not under your control

_____

Workbook for the Practice of Self-Assertiveness

NLP techniques – Look at the following example questions and answer honestly:

If you had to make a choice between going to a party and completing your project report, due tomorrow, which would you choose? Why?

If you have to choose between a boring but honest and upright man and a handsome and dashing man who is a liar and cheater, who will you choose and why?

Affirmations – Complete the following self-assertiveness affirmations in your own words:

1) I am

_____

2) I am not deterred by

_____

3) I stand up for

_____

Visualization – Recall a particularly difficult situation that keeps recurring in your life in which you find it tough to say no. Now, visualize this situation in your mind and imagine confidently saying no. Make detailed notes of your imagination including the choice of words, body language, gestures, tone of voice, etc.

___

Workbook for the Practice of Living With Purpose

NLP techniques – Write down three of your most important life goals, ensuring all of them fulfill the SMART goal requirement:

- S – Specific
- M – Measurable
- A – Achievable
- R - Realistic
- T – Timebound

Affirmations – Write down three affirmations that are aligned with your life's purpose:

1) _____

2) _____

3) _____

Visualization – Rate the following goals in order of the importance in your life:

- Completing an advanced course that will help in boosting your career
- Getting a promotion
- Earning lots of money

- Traveling the world
- Following a favorite hobby

Now, for the first three goals, imagine you have achieved the successful outcome as per your desires. Write down the visuals in detail. Don't hesitate to make your own goals if none of the above match your desires.

Workbook for the Practice of Personal Integrity

NLP techniques – Look at the following examples of how to say no politely. Practice them regularly. In fact, you can use them as affirmations for daily practice. Remember the importance of learning to say no to ensure you make only those promises you can keep.

- I am afraid this is not a good fit for me
- Sounds very interesting, but at present, I'm really pressed for time
- I am sorry, but I have to pass up your invitation this time.
- If I agree to help you simply because you are insisting on it, I will be making a false promise
- Sorry, this does not fit my present schedule

Affirmations – Create three affirmations for personal integrity:

1) _____

2) _____

3) _____

Meditation – Use all of the above affirmations to meditate on daily.

Maintaining a diary – Think of two of the most difficult times in your life when you broke promises to people you loved and cared for. Now, answer the following questions:

Why did you break the promise?

_____

What were your feelings?

_____

What were the lessons you learned which helped you improve your personal integrity?

_____

Chapter 6: Conclusion

Lisa Lieberman-Wang, the famous author of many self-help books, says, *"You are not your mistakes; they are what you did, not who you are."*

Building self-esteem is not an overnight exercise. It takes time and sustained efforts to build your self-esteem slowly and steadily. It is important for you to first make the decision to change yourself for the better. This crucial decision is the start of a long but fun journey. Don't worry if you initially face failures. Stumbling on the way is the best way to make your learning effective.

Continue to increase your self-awareness about the six components of self-esteem discussed in this book. Repeat the quizzes and questionnaires given here to keep track of your progress. The journey of building self-esteem may seem long and arduous, especially if you are a victim of low self-esteem. Don't be discouraged by the challenges you will encounter. Simply continue to persist, and make the development of the base components of self-esteem discussed in this book a lifelong effort.

This book is specifically targeted at women with low self-esteem. The self-assessment exercises and templates are given in this book are extremely useful to accurately gauge your current status, and then to build efficient plans to develop self-esteem.

Confidence, self-esteem, and assertiveness are all related and yet different from each other. The main focus of this book was on Self Esteem.

Read the books *for women* from Maria van Noord:

- Confidence for Women
- Assertiveness for Women

www.ingramcontent.com/pod-product-compliance
Lightning Source LLC
Chambersburg PA
CBHW072008110526
44592CB00012B/1241